Glass Fusing
Techniques

Wow! I can make that!

By April Calmelat

Copyright

Glass Fusing Techniques: Wow! I Can Make That!

Copyright ©2018 by April Calmelat

First Edition.

Books > Education & Reference > Crafts >Art Glass > Fusing

ISBN-13: 978-1720504894

ISBN-10: 172050487X

Photos and Illustrations by April Calmelat

Disclaimers:

Dedication

This comprehensive volume is gratefully dedicated to my comprehensive husband, Jake, who has been my total helpmate for over 40 years.

Table of Contents

Introduction: Why Fuse Glass?

My husband once said to me, "Glass can cut you. A kiln can burn you. Who wouldn't want to learn fusing?" He had a point, but I was fascinated anyway by the spectacular results one can achieve if willing to accept the dangers.

This beautiful, unfriendly substance has challenged and captivated me for over 20 years. I'm hooked.

Part I: Fusing Basics

Chapter 1: The Kiln and Glass Fusing

1. Kiln Basics

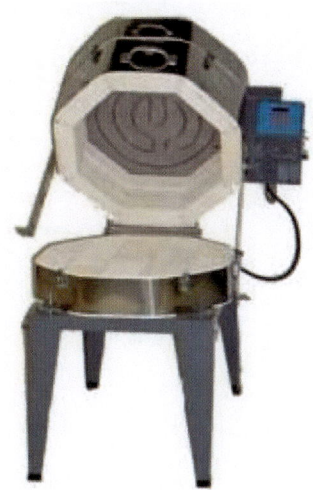

Clam Shell Kiln for Glass Fusing

Learning to work the kiln is fun, if sometimes scary. Today's glass kilns have come a long way from the big old ceramics kiln I learned to fuse glass on. Either type of kiln works, but the kiln built for glass is easier. The principle difference between the two types of kilns is that the kiln for glass has electric coils in the lid. The kiln for ceramics also works well as long as it is electric, has an electronic controller built in.

Some glass kilns are quite small, such as those used in jewelry making. Other studio kilns are big enough for large projects or multiple concurrent student projects to be fused. Some glass kilns have the barrel on the top (shown above) and others have it on the bottom. They all work for fusing, though some of the more advanced techniques are easier with one type than another.

If you plan to do any glass combing or other high temperature techniques, your kiln should have 240 volts also. Small electric glass kilns which operate on

110 volts do not usually have enough power to reach the high temperatures above 1600 degrees Fahrenheit. These kilns are fine for basic fusing, however.

2. Kiln Programming

Kilns with an electronic controller all work in generally the same way. The newest kilns have a few permanent programs which make it easy to fuse most things. I have found that as my glass types, thicknesses and techniques vary, the programs already stored in the kiln's computer don't really suit my needs. This means I need to develop my own programs.

Have you ever put boiling hot gelatin into a non-Pyrex bowl? What happened? Often the glass bowl cracks or breaks. This is due to glass stress. If you raise or lower the temperature of the kiln too quickly, a similar result will happen.

Glass stress and strain topics are discussed in Chapter 2. In order to prevent your art piece from cracking or breaking, certain heating concepts are important to remember.

The kiln speed at which you raise the temperature as well as that used in cooling the glass must follow certain guidelines. Generally, the temperature must be raised slowly up to the point where the glass is liquid enough that it will no longer break. After the peak temperature is reached, the glass must be cooled slowly enough that when it starts to solidify again, it will not develop stress and break.

The heat-cool cycle should look something like this:

1. Slow heat up to about 1000 degrees Fahrenheit
2. Fast heat up to working temperature
3. Fast cool down to about 1000 degrees
4. Slow the speed down from 1000 to 900 degrees to let the glass catch up with the kiln
5. Hold the kiln steady around 900 degrees to soak the glass (annealing)

Note: You cannot anneal too much, but you can anneal too little.

6. Slow cool down to room temperature

With the advent of electronic kiln programmers, it is easy to develop your own kiln programs. The kiln will come with specific instructions on how to program it. Generally, you first determine the program number and the number of ramps you want for your fusing cycle. Next you will determine the speed for the first ramp and the desired maximum temperature. Then you decide if you want to hold the glass (also called soaking the glass) at that maximum temperature, and if so, for how long. When these three things are entered, the program will ask you about the second ramp, maximum temperature, any hold you may want, and so on until you have programmed all the ramps. When cooling the kiln, just program the desired temperature to be lower instead of higher at the end of the ramp.

The kiln program will look something like this (This is only an example):

- Program #1

- Ramps: 5

- Ramp 1: 300 degrees/hour

- Temperature: 1000 degrees

- Hold: 30 minutes

- Ramp 2: 700 degrees/hour

- Temperature: 1500 degrees

- Hold: 5 minutes

- Ramp 3: 9999/hour or AFAP (as fast as possible)

- Temperature: 1000 degrees

- Hold: 0 minutes

- Ramp 4: 150 degrees/hour

- Temperature: 900 degrees

- Hold: 1:25 (1 hour and 25 minutes)

- Ramp 5: 300 degrees/hour

- Temperature: 300 degrees

- Hold: 0 minutes

- Alarm: If desired.

- Delay start: This needs to be set at the beginning. Follow manufacturer's directions.

- Cplt: Program is complete.

<u>Do NOT open the kiln until it is back to room temperature or about 150 degrees at most.</u>

3. Basic Fusing: What Takes Place

Glass pieces placed on a base piece of clear glass before fusing.

Glass pieces on a clear base after full fusing at 1500 degrees Fahrenheit. This makes what I call a "pancake."

Glass pieces on a clear base after slumping the fused pancake into a bowl mold.

4. Working the Kiln

You will want to fire your beautiful glass art pieces at different temperatures depending upon the grand scheme you have in mind. If you want the piece of art to have a flat surface at the finish, it needs to be hotter than if you want the piece to have texture. Generally, in order to make the upper pieces lose their edge definition and become completely flat with the lower glass, you will need to take the kiln temperature up to 1500 degrees Fahrenheit or a little bit more.

Flat fused at 1500 degrees Fahrenheit.

Suppose you would like to retain definition of the edges on the top piece of glass to create depth and texture. Obviously, you need to set your kiln to reach a lower top temperature in order to just barely attach the top glass onto the base glass. Two pieces won't stick together at temperatures much below 1400 degrees, so this is the lowermost temperature for glass fusing. Fused glass which leaves the edge texture is called tack fusing. Other processes, like bending glass into or over molds, are done at even lower temperatures when you aren't trying to stick two pieces of glass together.

Tack Fused at 1400 degrees Fahrenheit

5. What Kiln Program(s) Should I Use?

The answer, of course, is it depends. It depends on what you have in mind for your piece of art glass. Are you just melting the pieces together, or do you have some grand scheme for the finished piece? I remember a story my father, a medical school dean, once told a group of young graduating doctors. It went something like this:

A man in medieval times was walking along the road one day when he encountered another man carrying a hod full of stones on his shoulder. As he approached the carrier he asked, "What are you doing?"

"I'm carrying stones," the burdened man responded.

"I see." The man said and continued on his way. A short while later he came upon another man also with stones heading down the road. He asked him, "What are you doing?"

"Building a wall," the stone carrier replied.

"Yes," he thought. Shortly thereafter, he came upon a third stone carrier and asked him the same question, "What are you doing?"

"I'm building a cathedral," he said.

There are three ways to develop your kiln program:

1. Read literature which will tell you how fast or slow to make the ramps as well as stop and hold temperatures. There are numerous books and websites which detail explicit outlines for kiln programs.

2. Experiment on your own. This is the method I have used for many years. Unfortunately, for me, I am not a particularly good guesser and have had any number of failures because my kiln settings were wrong.

3. Read what others recommend and then modify it to your own kiln's eccentricities as well as to meet your own desired effects.

6. Kiln parts failure.

A kiln is a tool, and as such, it will wear out over time with repeated use. Often, the kiln can be repaired, thus preventing another big monetary investment in buying a replacement. Fire bricks, thermocouples, coils, whole control boxes, shelves, and kiln posts are all replaceable from online sources. It costs far less to replace a single part than to buy a whole new kiln. After twenty years of kiln use, I had to replace my thermocouple recently, and it only cost about $75. But be sure to get good installation instructions or hire an electrician!

****

"Even small, menial tasks can lead to greatness in glass art, as in other endeavors, if you have the courage to think big. (And, it takes a lot of stones to make a cathedral!)"

Chapter 2: What is Fused Glass?

1. Different Types of Glass Used in Fusing

There are several different types of glasses commonly used in fusing. Transparent, or cathedral, glass is most often used in stained glass windows as it lets the most light through. When I was a teenager, my father took my family and me to see the cathedrals of Europe. I was amazed by the stunning windows made of this colored glass. I confess, the art galleries he dragged us all (seven of us) to eventually became tiresome (so many Hogarths). I never grew tired of the gorgeous stained glass windows of the huge churches, however. Transparent glass is fantastic when used in a fused piece set on a window sill or elsewhere so that the light hits it from the back. It often looks dark when lit from the front, though.

Opalescent glass is also commonly used in fusing. This glass is not clear and although light does come through it somewhat, you cannot see through it. Opalescent glass is usually best viewed from the front. This dichotomy between transparent and opalescent glasses is something to consider when selecting the glass for your art piece.

To add to your confusion, some glass has both opalescent and transparent glass in the same sheet! Whatever glasses you select for your piece, make sure the different pieces are compatible in their coefficients of expansion! (More about this later.)

2. Glass Brands

Virtually any glass can be fused, but not with just any other glass. The problem arises when the fused glasses used don't expand in the same way. When this happens, your fused piece will crack or break at some point.

This can be heartbreaking, so in order to avoid tears or profanities, *ALWAYS* use glasses which are compatible with each other. Some brands of glass have whole lines of compatible glasses in different colors, thicknesses, and transparencies.

In America, probably the biggest seller for fusing is Bullseye CoE90 glass. Uroboros, Wasserman and Spectrum also have compatible lines. One brand may not be compatible with another, so check the compatibility before making a piece with differing brands. Because I am not familiar with European or other regions' brands, I would advise fusers in other countries to check with their glass suppliers to be sure the glasses they buy are compatible.

3. What Fusing Means

The most basic concept in fusing is to melt one piece of glass hot enough so it sticks, or fuses, to another piece of glass. You can start with any compatible base glass and simply scatter pieces of glass on top and get a charming piece of fused art.

Most of my glass fusing has centered on making plates and bowls, however, though sometimes a plaque says it all. Usually, I like to make things that are, at least hypothetically, functional. When making a fused plate or bowl where the pieces will fit together like a jigsaw puzzle, the most elementary steps I use are as follows:

a. Have an idea of what I want to make.

b. Draw a picture or find one in a pattern book. (Stained glass pattern books can be used for fusing too, but I like to make my own designs.)

c. Enlarge or reduce the drawing to make a paper pattern exactly the size I want (i.e. to fit the mold).

d. Make and cut out enough copies of the pattern to make it easy to stick pattern pieces onto the glass and then cut them out without destroying your only complete pattern.

e. Select my glass for the project.

f. Stick the paper pattern pieces to the glass you plan to use. (Water soluble glue sticks work well.)

g. Cut the glass pieces out, then lay them on a base piece of glass.

h. Fuse the pieces to the base glass in the kiln. This makes a flat piece which I call a "pancake."

i. Slump the flat pancake onto a mold.

****

Chapter 3: What is Compatible Glass?

In order to fuse glass successfully, it is important to understand the concept of compatibility. When two different glasses have the same coefficient of expansion, they are usually compatible and can be fused together successfully..

Collection of compatible glasses

1. Expansion Coefficients Explained (the math of fusing)

All solids expand or contract with the application of heat or cold. Glass is no exception. The degree to which heat causes glass to expand depends upon how tightly the molecules of glass are held together. Loosely bonded glass molecules will expand with heat (or retract with cold) a bit more than tightly bound glass molecules. To the naked eye, it all looks like glass, but on a molecular level, differing glasses are quite different.

When trying to fuse two glasses together, they must have similar molecular expansion properties in order to adhere to one another. If the expansion properties are different, the glasses will not fuse properly, and will be stressed in the process. This will cause the fused glass to crack or break.

The degree to which any given glass will expand is measured in inches for each inch of glass per degree of increase in temperature. This change is very small and is shown as the number of inches times 10^{-7} (e.g. 90×10^{-7}). When referring to the coefficient of expansion, the notation of 10^{-7} is omitted, however. The remaining number is called the coefficient of expansion or CoE (e.g. 90).

COEFFICIENTS OF EXPANSION FOR MOST GLASSES (CoE)
From Published Data

Brand/Type of Glass	Coefficient of Expansion
Moretti (Effetre) rods and sheet glass	104
Spectrum Compatible	96
Uroboros Compatible 96	96
Bullseye Compatible 90	90
Uroboros Compatible 90	90
Wasserman Compatible 90	90
Float (window and most bottle) glass	Variable 83-87
Pyrex (borosilicate)	32.5

2. Glass Stress and Strain (the science of fusing)

Everyone knows that hot glass that is suddenly immersed in cold water will likely shatter (except borosilicate Pyrex™ with its very tight molecular bonds). Most glass develops stress both when it is rapidly heated and when it is cooled rapidly. Enough stress will cause it to shatter.

Glass develops stress (tension across the area) as it strains (expands) when heated. The glass molecules are bonded together, but heating makes the bonds wiggle. Think of the bonds like rubber bands holding the glass molecules together. When the glass is cool, the rubber bands move gently and uniformly, but when heated, the rubber bands begin to stretch and vibrate rapidly. The hotter the glass, the more the bonds dance. As the glass heats up, its exposed surfaces may heat or cool faster or slower than the inner regions. This means that the molecules move non-uniformly and develop tension between the hotter and cooler areas. The bonds become tense as they stretch. If they strain enough, the stress becomes so great that the bonds break. Unless the temperature is hot enough, this causes the glass to shatter.

If heating is done slowly, eventually all the bonds begin to vibrate uniformly once again. The vibration is intense, but stress and strain disappear. When the glass becomes hot enough that the bonds are all broken, the glass becomes liquid.

All glass has strain and stress temperatures. When glass cools from the fusing point, care must be taken to allow time for the molecules to slow down and begin to move uniformly again. Annealing is the holding or soaking of the glass at a certain temperature long enough for the non-uniform strain and stress to disappear. The best temperature for annealing varies from one glass to another but is usually somewhere between 960°F down to 930°F for most fusible glass.

Generally, about a half hour for each thickness of glass will safely anneal most glass, but the width of the glass is also a factor. The total amount of glass must be considered. Glass sitting in a mold also adds time to the heating or cooling. Glass cannot be over-annealed. Soak the glass as long as feasible to allow the glass molecules to become quiet. After annealing, reduce the temperature slowly to prevent stress from recurring as the piece gradually cools to room temperature.

Thermal Stress and Strain of Glass Molecules

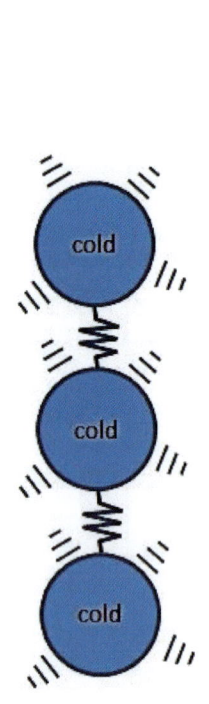

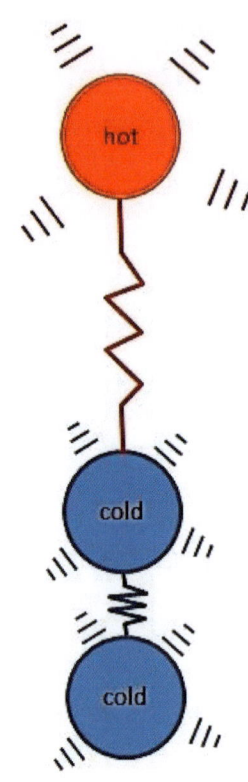

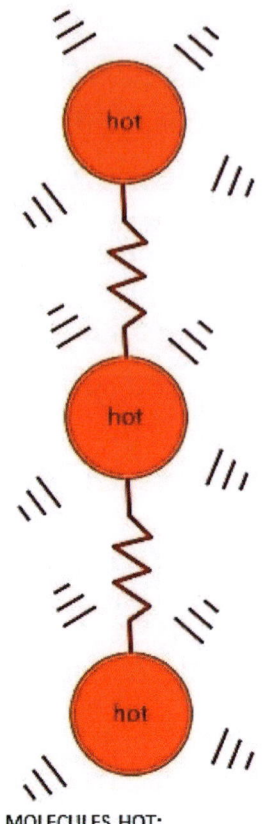

ALL MOLECULES COLD:
- Uniform wiggling
- Bonds stretch (strain) uniformly
- Bonds not overstressed
- Glass very solid

SOME MOLECULES HOT, SOME COLD:
- Hot bonds wiggle more aggressively
- Bonds do not stretch (strain) uniformly
- High tension between hot and cold
- Hot weaker bonds can break resulting in glass cracking

ALL MOLECULES HOT:
- Hot bonds wiggle more aggressively
- Bonds stretch (strain) uniformly
- All bonds weakened but not overstressed
- With enough heat glass becomes liquid

3. Kiln Program Basics: Soaking the Glass

Because glass can develop stress both as it is heated and as it cools, multiple ramp speeds allow the fuser to raise the temperature slowly then go much faster after the stress is gone. Then the fuser can cool it as fast as possible until the stress returns; hold the glass for a while at a constant temperature to anneal it to remove any remaining stress, and finally slowly cool it off back down to room temperature.

The bigger and thicker the glass you are fusing is, the slower you will need to both heat and cool your piece. Generally, for two or three thicknesses of glass, raising the temperature of the kiln about 300 degrees per hour is safe. At just under 1000 degrees the stress disappears. The glass is so soft that it can't break. Keep in mind that the glass temperature is always about 50 degrees behind the kiln temperature whether the temperature is rising or falling. So, on the rise, when the kiln reaches 1000 degrees, the artist can speed up the ramp to the highest desired fusing temperature.

Occasionally you may want to hold the glass at the peak temperature to further the fuse. Obviously, it is important to monitor your kiln closely. It is important to be safe when using the kiln. The temperatures attained inside a kiln will easily ignite a careless fuser.

The most critical time to use the soak or hold option on the kiln is during the cooling phase. From the top temperature of 1400 – 1500 degrees it is safe to cool the fused piece as quickly as possible down to about 1000 degrees. Ramp down slowly from 1000°F to the anneal temperature. The glass is still soft but it stiffens up again somewhere around 930 degrees whereupon stress again becomes a factor. Treat the glass carefully. GO SLOWLY. Setting the ramp to cool down at 150 degrees per hour from 1000 degrees to 930 is usually safe. When the kiln reaches 930, soak it there for an hour or more depending on how thick the glass is and whether or not it is sitting in a mold. This soak anneals the glass and removes the stress. Remember, the more mass to cool down, the longer it takes. For two or three layers of glass on the kiln shelf without a mold, a hold at 930 Fahrenheit for one and a half to one and three quarters hours is adequate. If the same glass is in a mold, soak the glass for two hours or longer.

After the soak to anneal the piece, avoid having a perfectly fused piece shatter by setting the kiln to restart cooling down very slowly from 930°F. Ramp it down at about 150-200 degrees per hour until it reaches 300°F. The kiln program is then complete. But don't open up the kiln yet! Wait to open it up until the glass is cool enough to handle easily without gloves, i.e. below 150 degrees, whereupon you can open up the kiln to see your results.

4. How to tell if your glass is compatible

For quite a while, the only way to tell if two pieces of glass had a compatible CoE was to try fully fusing little samples of the glasses together and see if they had stress. The stress is seen by examining the fused glass with a polarized light and a filter.

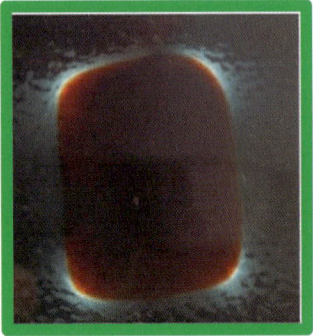

The white halo areas are evidence of stress due to incompatibility. Float window glass was fused to CoE90 glass in this example.

Light will shine brightly at the junction of the two glasses if stress is present. Stressometer gadgets with polarized lenses are available to reveal the stress. This process is time consuming and uses up expensive glass, however.

Another method is to fuse two strips of different glasses together. Then, using a gas torch, pull the ends of the fused strip apart until it breaks. Watch what happens next. If the glass curls up, the two glasses are not compatible. If it stays straight, they are. This process is tricky and easy to misread.

Early on in my fusing career, I tried to save money by purchasing Bullseye glass that was red labeled. This red labeled glass was from the manufacturing run adjacent to the batch which tested compatible. It was usually compatible too, but not always. Most of my problems related to yellow glass from the red labeled run, but that may have been coincidence.

Over the past twenty years I have heard the heartbreaking sound of "plink" more times than I want to remember. The plink sound happens when your lovely finished piece suddenly and irrevocably cracks because of incompatibility between glasses. It can happen during firing in the kiln or much later as your finished work sits on the window sill. A sip of something distilled is helpful at these times.

Unfortunately, incompatibility is not a fixable problem. When it happens, your glass is toast. The best defense is a good offense. Buy only compatible glass **all the time**. If you combine brands it is possible problems may arise with compatibility, though I have not experienced this personally. Because I began my glass collection with it, I always buy CoE90 glass and fuse both Bullseye and Uroboros brands together.

****

"Incompatibility exists in glass as much as it does in people. If the bonds are loose in one and tight in the other, stress will result and the union will break."

Chapter 4: Tools for Fusing Success

1. Safety First

Broken or hot glass easily causes injury and must therefore be handled carefully. Duh. Broken glass is pretty obvious. You must take care when moving broken glass into the trash can. Also be careful when you take the trash bag out of the can as the glass can poke through.

The problem with hot glass is it looks just like cool glass. For this reason, when working with hot glass, it is helpful to keep an eye on the kiln thermostat to see how hot it is. Remember, the glass inside is actually probably either roughly 50 degrees hotter or cooler than the kiln depending on whether you have been heating or cooling when you want to open it. For this reason, when your piece is finished, wait until it reaches no hotter than 150 degrees Fahrenheit before you open the kiln. Also, this prevents thermal shock and breaking of the glass.

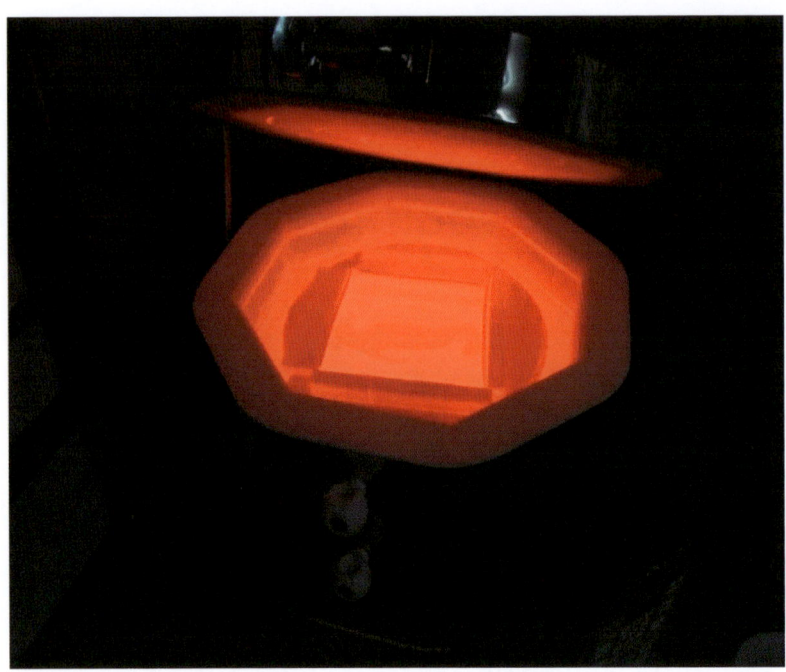

Some fusing techniques require you to open the kiln when it is hot. As the kiln temperature rises, sudden temperature changes, such as opening the kiln lid can cause thermal shock to the glass. Above roughly 950 degrees the glass is liquid enough not to be shocked when you open the lid. I always wait until the kiln registers at least 1000 degrees before opening the top as the temperature falls dramatically when I do open it.

A very hot kiln requires special safety protection when opened. I remember my first time combing glass. My eyebrows got a bit frizzled. Lesson learned. The special protection suggested is noted in the chapter on combing, but remember, anytime you open a hot kiln you should protect your eyes with didymium safety glasses and heavy Kevlar-type gloves. You will need even more protection if you plan to work with the glass in the hot kiln rather than just observe it.

Priority #1: If you ever plan to open the kiln while it is hot, you should always wear **Didymium glasses** to protect your eyes.

Priority #2: Very long **Kevlar Gloves** or other high heat resistant gloves are mandatory when handling a hot kiln handle, hot glass, or tools in the hot kiln.

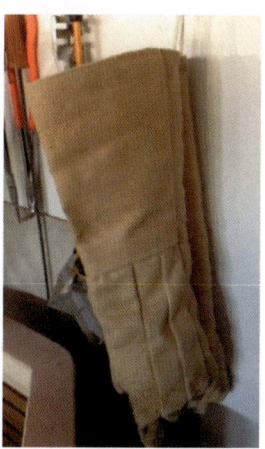

A **Face Shield** for protection if opening the kiln when working the glass at a very high temperature (over 1500 degrees) will keep your eyebrows and nose from burning. This is especially important when combing glass. Long cotton sleeves, (no polyester as it may stick to the skin if heated) and a leather apron or other heat resistant clothing is also advisable when combing glass.

Sound Protectors will save your hearing when using electric saws, drills, or grinders.

2. Cutting Tools

Glass Cutter

In addition to having the use of a kiln, fusing requires compatible glass, and at minimum, some kind of glass cutter. Glass cutters don't actually cut the glass, rather they score a small crack it in which allows the artist to break the glass along the score line.

Finger grip style glass cutter

The finger grip style cutter has a built in cutting oil reservoir which allows smooth cuts for many years without becoming dull. Some people prefer the simpler glass cutter shown below.

3. Breaking Tools

Grozer Pliers

Grozers bite glass off. They are wonderful for curves, especially those inside curves you want to break off. I have found that putting the edge of the grozer right up next to the score line, but not on it, and pulling away from the main body of glass works best on those difficult inside curves. Some grozers have ridges to help grip the glass. These also work well to gently bite edges off small areas of glass. They are no substitute for the glass grinder, but they cut down on how much grinding you need to do.

Ridges grip the glass.

Running Pliers

Running Pliers were a terrific invention. They have a slightly curved area where the pliers meet the glass which causes it to split the glass along a straight score line. They aren't much good for curves, however, but with practice you can do some slight curving with them. But boy oh boy, they are great for old arthritic hands that need a straight line broken in the glass!

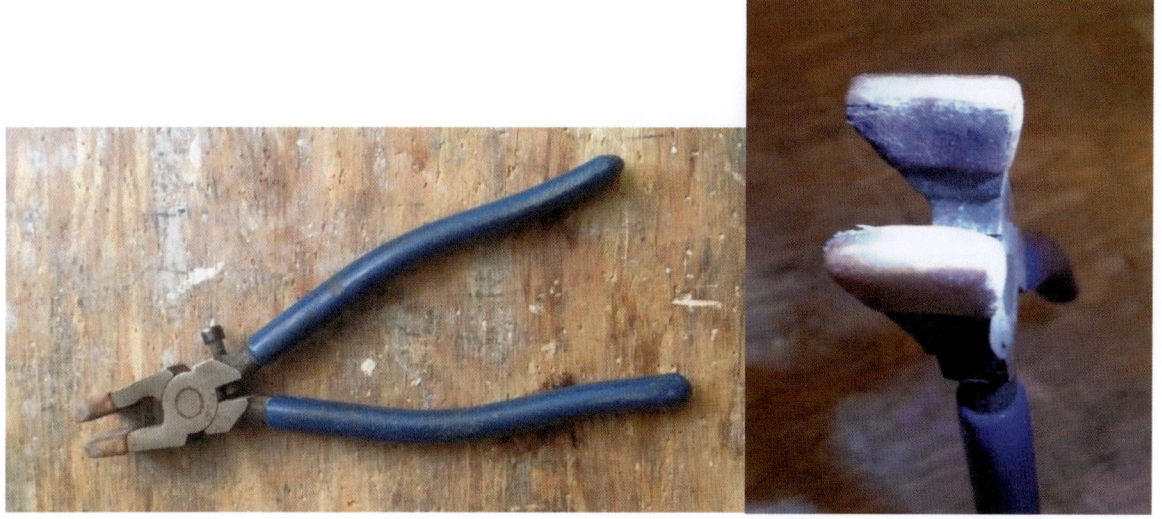

Running pliers have curves which help split the glass in a straight line.

4. Grinding Tools

Because curves are so lovely, it is important to have a way to make them easily. Grinding tools do the job. They also allow you to smooth off jagged edges to refine the finish on your work. The grinder works well to remove little spicules of glass on the edges of pieces which have been fused to 1450 degrees or above and to remove sharp corners on squares and rectangles. Most glass fusers begin with a simple electric glass grinder and move on to more elaborate tools as their skills develop.

Electric Glass Grinders are commonly used in stained glass and fused glass work.

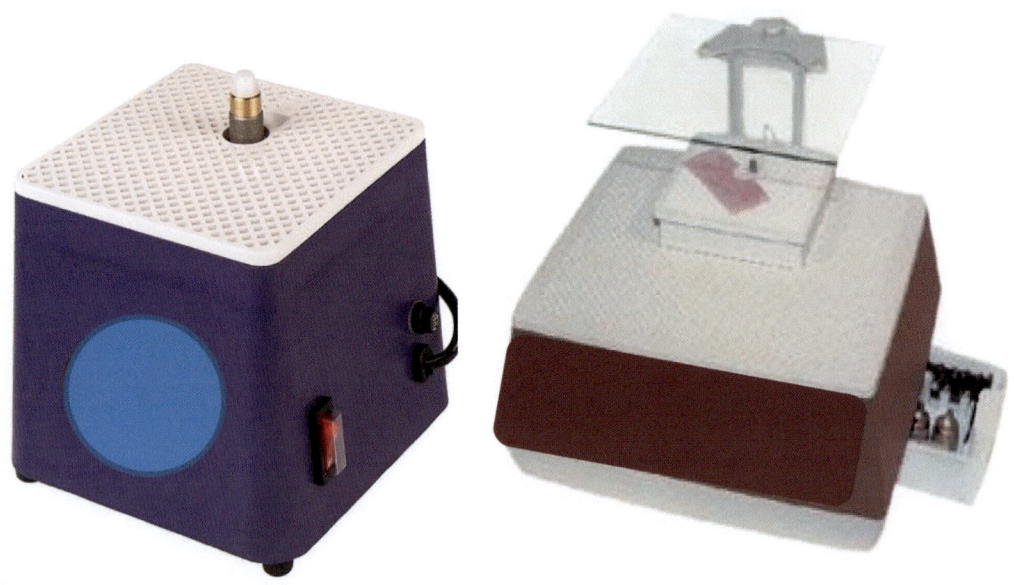

Electric Glass Grinders

Wet Ring Saw for Glass

The wet ring saw is a boon to both stained glass window makers and fusers alike. This saw consists of a motor connected to a diamond-coated, ring-shaped saw blade which rotates around and picks up water from the tub below with every rotation. Because the ring blade is diamond coated on all sides, it is easy to make cuts from any direction. This would be impossible with a hand held cutter or even a band saw for glass. You can run the glass in curves, inside cuts, the sky is the limit! By the way, I gave up my band saw immediately when I got my first ring saw. The band saw works relatively well in one direction, and with practice you can turn corners with it, but it is much more difficult to use than the ring saw. I highly recommend getting a ring saw if you are serious about working with glass. The only drawbacks to this saw are that it is slower than breaking glass by hand and the saw plus replacement parts are moderately expensive.

 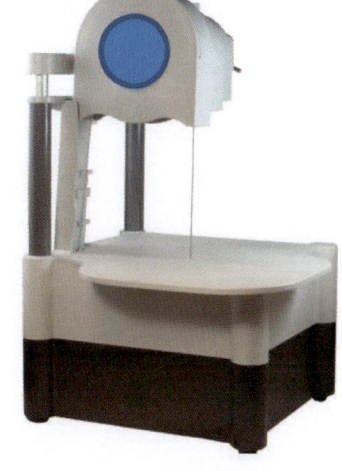

Wet Ring Saw   **Wet Band Saw for glass**

Wet Tile Saw

A tile saw is made to cut ceramic and porcelain tiles but also works well to cut glass. For best results when cutting glass, you will need to put a diamond edged blade on it rather than the carbide blade it probably comes with. Hardware stores carry these saws and blades. To cut glass, the tile saw should have a reservoir of water to keep the saw blade and glass from getting too hot.

Although I have used my tile saw to cut a lot of ceramic tile for various home improvement projects, my favorite thing to do is to use it to cut glass. I can cut straight lines in thick, already fused glass that would be impossible to cut otherwise. It is a great tool if to have you are serious about fusing.

Wet Saw for Tiles

Electric Drill

An electric drill with bit for glass or ceramics is handy if you want to put holes in the glass. Remember to keep the drill bit cool with water or oil to protect the glass from breaking.

Electric Drill

5. Release agents

Whenever glass is heated in the kiln, a release agent such as high fire kiln wash *must* be used to prevent the glass sticking to the shelf or mold.

There are a few different types of release agents. Which one you choose depends upon the mold or shelf you are using. Release agents are discussed in more detail in Chapter 9.

6. Miscellaneous Tools

Bandages are essential to have handy when working with glass. Always think about what you can do to make the process safer and you may avoid getting more than a little glass cut or two.

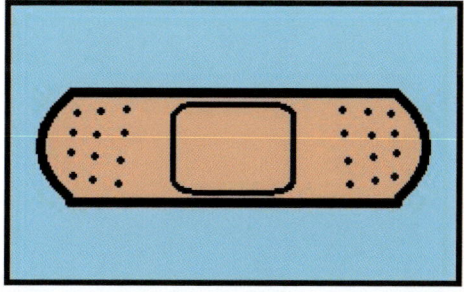

An **Abrasive Block helps to** smooth rough edges after fusing.

Glue or hairspray works to stick slippery glasses together before fusing. Some glass manufacturers sell special glue for use on glass, but my favorite is inexpensive, water-based hairspray. I find it sticks gently, not permanently, but enough to hold things steady and burns completely leaving no residue after fusing.

If white glue is used, it should be minimal. Apply it with a toothpick only to the outer edges or corner of the glass. This allows the glue to burn off. If too much glue is used, an unattractive brown or white residue will remain after fusing. Never put glue under the center of the glass as it will leave a bump where it could not escape and burn off.

Computer Pattern Resizer software to make the design fit the mold size is a boon if available.

Molds

If three-dimensional pieces are desired, you will need some kind of mold. See Chapter 8 for more information on molds and their specific uses.

Mosaics Nippers

Nippers make little crescent shaped nips in glass. I have used them for mosaics many times, but they will not cut a straight line. For straight lines, breaking by hand or using the running pliers is best.

Scissors are helpful to cut out design patterns, cut fiber blanket etc.

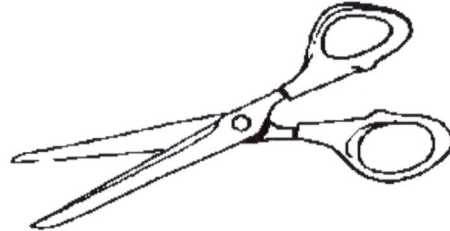

A **Waffle Board** is nice for making straight edges and as well as multiple pieces exactly the same size. A popular one is the Morton Board.

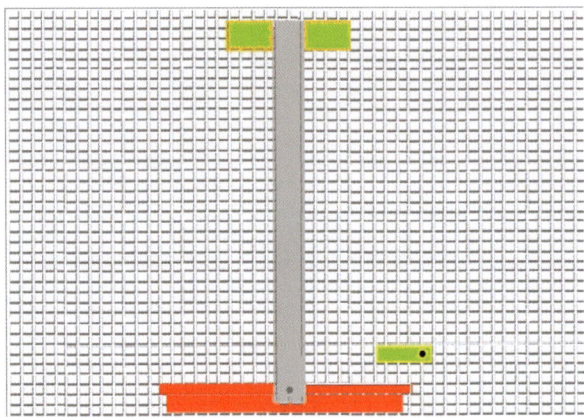

Pens, Pencils, Measuring tools and Paper for making patterns, drawing designs, measuring sizes etc. are important tools for any fuser.

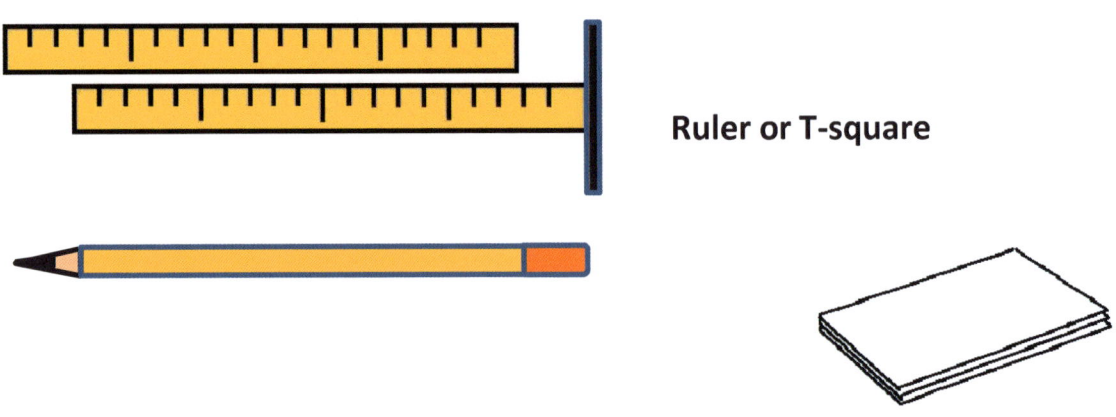

Ruler or T-square

The *most* important tool: A Creative Idea

＊＊＊＊＊＊＊＊＊＊＊＊＊＊＊＊＊＊＊＊＊

"The expectations of life depend upon diligence; the mechanic that would perfect his work must first sharpen his tools."

Confucius

Chapter 5: Cutting Glass

If you have experience cutting glass, you can skip this chapter. It is really intended for first time glass artists or those who want to review problem areas.

1. Cutting Straight Lines

Cutting glass in straight lines is relatively easy. For a medium sized piece of glass, press the cutter firmly on the glass and run it along to score the line. Then while holding the glass on either side of the scored line, rotate your hands away and downwards. The glass will break in most instances (but not all). After scoring large pieces of glass, hold the shorter side over the edge of the workbench or other long straight edge with both hands. Lift up the hanging glass and whack it down on the workbench edge. The glass should break along the score lines (usually). Already fused glass is much harder to break. For thick previously fused glass a wet tile saw makes straight lines a breeze.

2. Curves

Cutting curves can be very tricky using only a handheld cutter. All but the most gentle curves will need an electric grinder at least. Except for the handheld glass cutter, nearly all glass cutting equipment is coated with diamond dust. Although industrial diamonds are used, diamonds make the tools more expensive, unfortunately.

If you plan to cut circles or other curves, you will need a grinder, at minimum. A Taurus or similar wet ring saw will make curves easy because you can cut/grind the glass in any direction.

To make the edge of a thick fused circle smooth, try taking a short nail with a very big head (or better, a rose petal stand for making cake frosting) and put double sticky foam tape on the head and stick it to the middle of the glass circle. Poke the nail part through one of the holes on your electric grinder so that the edge of your glass just hits the grinder bit. As the grinder bit turns, gradually turn your glass around the attached spindle in the hole. The glass will be ground off the edge. Note: An attachment like this is available in the Taurus wet ring saw accessories package, but the ring saw cannot grind very thick glass. This little gray plastic nail has paid for itself a hundred times over in my studio.

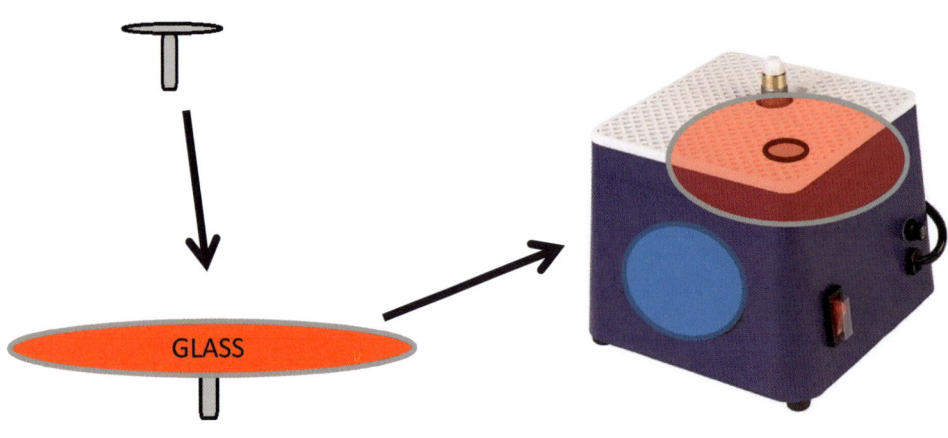

GLASS

3. Jigsaw puzzle shapes

Cutting out puzzle-like pieces is the same as cutting curves. Your glass size will be limited by the wet ring saw size, but otherwise, curves of any kind are pretty much unfettered.

****

"Cultivate your curves - they may be dangerous but they won't be avoided."

Mae West

Chapter 6: Color and Heat Considerations

1. Opalescent Glass

It is hard to see through opalescent glass as it is opaque. This feature has both advantages and disadvantages in fusing.

Opalescent glass tends to melt at a very slightly higher temperature than transparent glass. This is usually not very significant, but when opalescent glass is fused along with transparent, the transparent may spread out a bit more. Different colors also melt slightly differently from each other as well.

When overlapping opalescent glass on top of transparent, the color may change slightly, but most of the transparent glass will be hidden by the opalescent. Only when a bright light shines behind the piece will the transparent color be seen. For this reason, if you want to blend colors, in most cases, it is much better to put the transparent glass on top of the opalescent.

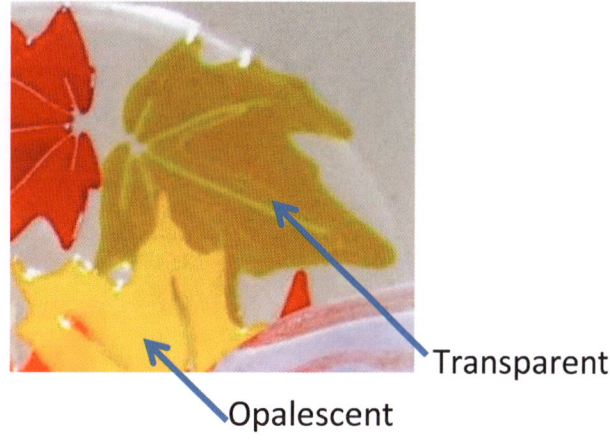

Transparent

Opalescent

The picture above shows an exception. Here the opalescent yellow glass is on top of the transparent yellow. If I had placed the transparent glass on the top, the opalescent glass leaf would have shown through.

2. Transparent Glass

Transparent glass is easy to see through, especially when light shines on it from behind. It is glorious to see on a window sill in the morning sun.

Transparent glass melts at a slightly lower temperature than opalescent and therefore, if you fuse a piece with both types of glass, the transparent color will likely expand more than the opalescent. The difference usually isn't big, but sometimes, it can surprise you.

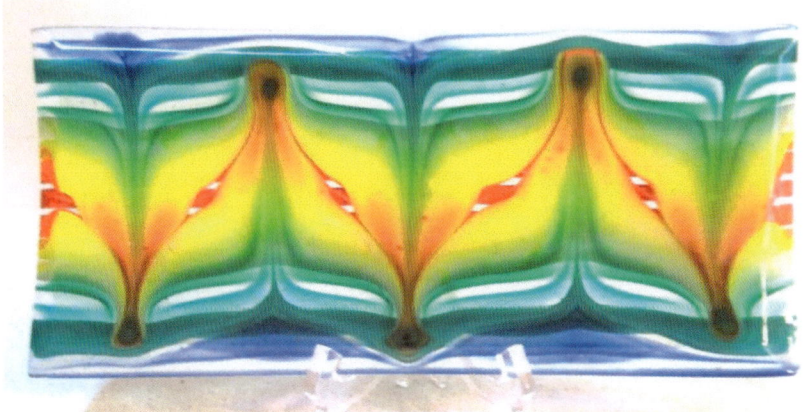

Surprise! The yellow and orange in this tray expanded a lot more than the other colors!

3. Adjacent Colors

Sometimes it is nice to separate colors with a bit of clear as seen between the blues and greens above. This makes the individual colors stand out for a more dramatic effect. Other times, especially if you are designing a picture, the closer the colors, the better your picture will look. Because as glass expands, it moves outward, two pieces next to each other may tend to separate a bit with fusing. If you truly want the pieces next to each other, consider overlapping them. Seen below are tack-fused hibiscus flowers with overlapping segments.

Sometimes, however, overlapping the glass is not the best choice.

Pale purple overlaps green stem here.

If you look closely, you can see that the stem of an orchid plant shows through the petals in this portion of a square tack-fused plate. While this is certainly an attractive plate, in a similar plate, the petals are joined by small stems to the main stem, thus preventing any overlaps or bleed through from the color underneath. The effect is improved.

4. Strikers

Sometimes glass changes color when heated. This is called striking. Bullseye used to make a steel blue color that turned silver when fused. Transparent yellow often turns gold (but not metallic). A light green may turn much darker when fused. For this reason, pay attention to the striker note on the glass label when you buy it. It might make a big change in your final piece from what you expect. If you don't know what color the striker glass will become, ask the sales person. They should know.

In the following pictures, the top color is before fusing and the bottom color is after fusing the same glass to 1500°F. This blue becomes a bit darker, the orange becomes red, the yellow becomes more golden and darker, and the pale pink becomes a deep opalescent salmon color.

Color charts showing the effects of color layering are available from glass companies for both opalescent (opaque) and transparent glass, or you can make your own.

5. Devitrification.

Devitrification is the gummy-looking white crystalized layer which happens when certain glasses remain too long at or above 1300 degrees Fahrenheit. It most commonly occurs during the cooling phase.

Solutions:

a. The devitrified layer can be removed with sand blasting or grinding on a lapidary disc. Apply a coating of overglaze or a layer of clear glass before refusing it to make a new surface. Be aware that some overglazes contain lead. Plates coated with this type of overglaze are not suitable for food.

b. The development of devitrification can also be avoided by placing a clear piece of glass on top of the colored glass.

c. Make a note to remember which particular glass devitrifies and should not be taken to temperature higher than 1300°F without an overglaze or cover glass.

d. In this case, I decided that the juxtaposition between the devitrified red glass and the unsullied black was a good thing. I left it alone.

****

Chapter 7: Planning Your Design

Before making a piece of fused glass art, it is helpful to know what you want to create. Since compatible stained glass is not cheap, it pays to plan your design. Are you making a glass painting? A graphic design? Will your piece have straight lines, curves, overlapping pieces, perforations? What colors will reveal your design best?

I usually draw a sketch of my fusing design before I begin. Sometimes it is very simple, as when just showing the pattern of my strokes before I comb glass. Other times, I draw out a whole picture with color to help me figure out what will look best. Still other times, I make a pattern which, when cut out, I place on the glass before I cut it.

What inspires me? Virtually anything can. Sometimes I see a picture in a book. Sometimes it is a snapshot I took. Other times, I get a glimpse of something I see on the internet and it compels me to try a similar technique. Inspiration can come from anywhere. You know it when you see it. It might even be something just from your own head!

A girlfriend of mine from long ago in high school mentioned that she wanted to put an horno (pronounced orno and roll the 'r' if you can) in her backyard. An horno is a type of outdoor chimney/fireplace where one can bake bread or pizzas and more. Hornos are very cool. As an Arizonan, I have seen hornos here from time as they were used traditionally by Native Americans and Hispanics. Inspiration hit me smack in the face! Below is the result.

I made this one by first drawing a pattern and then cutting out the pieces. I combined them into a sort of jigsaw puzzle which I placed on a white base glass before full fusing at 1500 degrees Fahrenheit. Before I slumped the flat glass into a plate mold, I first used a gold fusing pen to outline the individual parts for emphasis.

****

"Creativity is contagious, pass it on."
Albert Einstein

Chapter 8: Using Molds

1. Ceramic Molds

Fungi are molds, but not all molds are fungi. Ha. Ha. Molds are an essential part of the fusing process if you want to make something more than a flat plate. Molds turn your art piece into a functional item like a plate or a bowl. When you serve your appetizers to the crowd on top of your beautiful glass platter, expect to get as many, "Ahhs!" for the plate as for the food!

Several different types of molds can be used in the process of forming your art glass into shapes. Generally, it is difficult to slump glass into a very deep bowl or a tall vase. The glass just wants to sink down into the mold and often does so unevenly with one side sinking further than the other. This produces an uneven and often not beautiful result. Raising the temperature *slowly* will offer some measure of control, but if you want steep sides on your piece, it is more easily accomplished by draping the glass over the back side of a mold. However, when the backside is used, the glass often flutes and folds as it bends over the sides of the mold. Only by using a special drop out mold along with some cold work will you be able to make a steep-sided fused vase or cup.

Ceramic molds are very commonly used in fusing. Any clay bowl with gently sloped sides may be used in its bisque form before it is glazed. You can buy bisque at paint your own piece shops where you paint on the glaze and they fire it for you in their kiln. Bowls from these stores vary in price from a few dollars to about $100 each. If you buy a bisque bowl, you need to create a few very small holes in the lowest parts of the bottom to be sure no air is trapped beneath the glass when you fire it. I do this with a very small drill bit made for glass or ceramics in my electric drill. Put two to four tiny holes at the lowest points in the bowl. Don't worry; the glass won't ooze out of the holes. Next, paint the ceramic bisque bowl with mold release, and let it dry according to the directions on the release's label. Now you are ready to perch your pancake atop the mold and put it in the kiln.

Ceramic molds are also available from greenware stores used by ceramics hobbyists. Greenware is a clay piece which has not been fired yet at all. You will need to treat greenware very gently as it is quite easily broken. Since greenware is so very much cheaper than bisque, however, a little care can save you big dollars. You still need to make it into bisque, drill holes, and coat it with a release agent before using it as a glass mold. If you are careful and lucky, you can put the holes in it before you fire it into bisque. When firing greenware into bisque, you need to take the kiln up above glass fusing temperature to somewhere between 1800°F and 2000°F. The higher the temperature you take it, however, the harder and more vitrified the clay will become. This makes drilling the holes more difficult.

The most expensive place to buy a mold, which is truly a mold for glass, is the art glass or ceramics store. The advantage here is that it already is bisque, it already has the holes drilled into it, and it is nearly always suitable for slumping. All you need to do is apply a kiln release agent, and it is ready.

My husband, Jake, built these shelves to neatly store my molds. I didn't want to stack them as it would be harder to reach them out from under each other. I was also concerned about rubbing off the release agent if they were stacked. Since I am not only cheap, but also lazy, I wanted to make it unnecessary to reapply release agent to the molds very often.

2. Stainless Steel molds

Stainless steel bowls and cups can also be used for molds. (Do not try to use aluminum as its melting point is too low.) Formerly, the application of the release agent was tricky necessitating heating the mold and either air brushing or painting and sanding the release agent. It was a pain. Fortunately, not long ago, boron nitride mold release for metal molds became available in a spray can which is a huge advantage in making the coating smooth. The smoother the release coating, the smoother the inside of your glass will be. Be aware boron nitride is toxic, but it sprays on easily and can be reapplied when needed.

 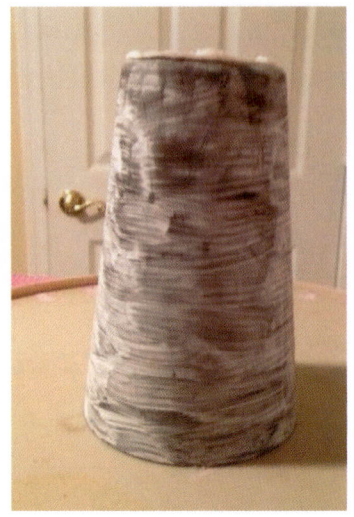

Both of these stainless steel molds are inverted cups. The one on the left, which I bought from a glass store, ironically, is not nearly as good as the cocktail shaker cup I bought at the kitchen store. They cost about the same. The mold on the left bows slightly as it is slightly smaller both at the top and at the bottom and bigger in the center. If the glass is hot enough and drapes far enough down the sides of this mold, it will get smaller at the bottom than in the middle. This will make it impossible to remove from the mold when the piece is cooled. This bowing is called an undercut. Undercuts must be avoided if you want to be able to remove your finished piece from the mold.

These pieces were squares draped over my cocktail shaker mold. You can see how folds are formed during draping. This effect is called a handkerchief. Please note, once kiln release has been painted on the cocktail shaker, it is 100% unsatisfactory for use in making cocktails. Release agents are not edible or drinkable.

Small, open handkerchiefs make lovely votive candle holders. I made this one to match my tablecloth.

3. Homemade molds

I had moderate success making molds with clay, but I thought making molds from dental stuff might be easier. I bought some mold material from a dental supply site I found online. The dental mold got hard almost immediately which made it hard to stir. It needed stirring, however, to make it less crumbly. I didn't have a lot of success with this process. Molds also can be made from plaster of Paris, but I have never tried.

Homemade mold from dental material: I called this one a square peg in a round hole. The mold fell apart after a couple of firings.

Red chili pepper drawer pull made in a homemade clay mold

4. Molds with Special Shapes

There are a number of different kinds of what I call specialty molds. I once took a taco salad bowl and covered it with clay to make a mold. I also made molds of various small, ceramic items I have around the house. Once I made a clay chili pepper and set it in mold making material to make a mold. From this mold, I made drawer pulls for my kitchen. The most common specialty molds are discussed here

Homemade mold from taco salad bowl: note air holes.

5. Drop out molds

Drop out molds are a fun way to make a bowl or plate which is tall and thin. Set the kiln program to go *slowly* so that the glass doesn't rush down and completely go through the hole in the mold. Place the mold on kiln posts to raise it up off the kiln shelf surface. Then put your glass on top and sag the glass through the hole. Be careful not to let the glass puddle on the shelf surface get too big to fit through the hole when the piece is cooled.

Drop out molds

Flower made in round drop out mold

Vases from drop out mold

6. Flower Molds

I get bored pretty easily and always want to try something new. Why make fifty of the same thing when I can experiment with new things all the time? The "expert" will have become an expert by making fifty of the same thing and becoming really, really good at that thing. I will never be so good at anything, but I think I have more fun always making my little experiments in glass. I really don't care if my art isn't perfect. I'm all about having a good time. In the past 20 years, I've had an awful lot of fun.

I decided a couple of years ago to try making flowers in three dimensions rather than just laying them flat on the surface of my bowl or plate. This is no easy task because of the complexities of fusing a deep design without having the folds you get when making a handkerchief. I found a mold that came in multiple pieces. The flowers were fused in separate pieces which were then pieced together with glue to become a flower

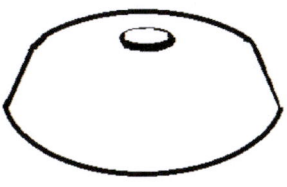 

Flower molds come in various shapes.

Multi-piece flowers

Irises rest in blown glass vase   Orchids glued to a copper tube

I didn't really enjoy using glue on my flowers. It seemed kind of like cheating to me (I have since gotten over this feeling and think whatever works is fine.). The glass fusing was supposed to do the sticking, not adding glue afterward. I looked around for another way to make three dimensional flowers. I found another multi-piece mold with petals which you lean against a small ceramic dome. Then you lay the already flatly fused, flower shaped piece on top of this multi-piece mold and drape it. It worked very well, though I had some trouble early on with the tips of the flower petals curling under instead of curving outward. A little less heat solved this problem. I found I could make the flower less open by raising the bigger dome up off the shelf with kiln posts.

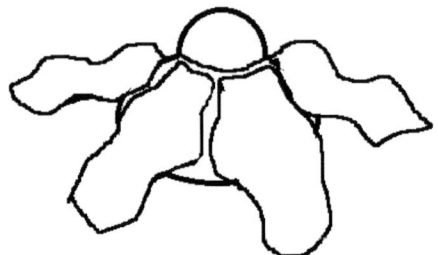

Multiple piece mold for flowers without glue

.

I have three chandeliers in my home which all had very ordinary glass shades on them. I thought flowers would be much better looking. I made these flowers with my multi-piece flower mold. Then, using my husband's drill press and a diamond drill bit with a big diameter, I cut holes in them for the light bulbs. I found my drill bit online, but I saw one for sale last week at a big box hardware store also. I love how each flower is different from the others, and each petal is different from the others too. This gives the piece a very handmade, original quality.

Dining room chandelier

I had a lot of fun making the lampshades. I made the base leaves different shades of green intentionally to give the lamp a more contemporary appearance.

7. Pitfalls with Molds

a. Glass is fused to a mold and cannot be unstuck.

Molds must have a layer of release coating to prevent the glass from sticking. High fire kiln primer is an excellent, inexpensive release agent for kilns, shelves, and ceramic molds. Different types exist but all are composed of finely ground minerals. Some of these agents wash off easily after one firing and others must be scraped off but last through several firings. Alternatively, a boron nitride release agent spray can be used on ceramic or steel molds. This is easy and convenient but more costly.

Screen melting and pot melting are exceptions where mold release is not used except on the receiving shelf. Although some glass will remain on the screen and pot, mold release should not be used as it may drip when the glass melts. In this case, the mold release will become a white residue in the glass.

The stainless steel screen is not coated with release, but the shelf underneath is. In this example, a one inch high circle of thin fiber blanket sits inside the ring at shelf level to prevent the glass from sticking to the stainless steel ring.

b. Glass stuck in mold undercuts.

It is imperative to check new molds for undercuts. An example of an undercut on a draping mold is shown here:

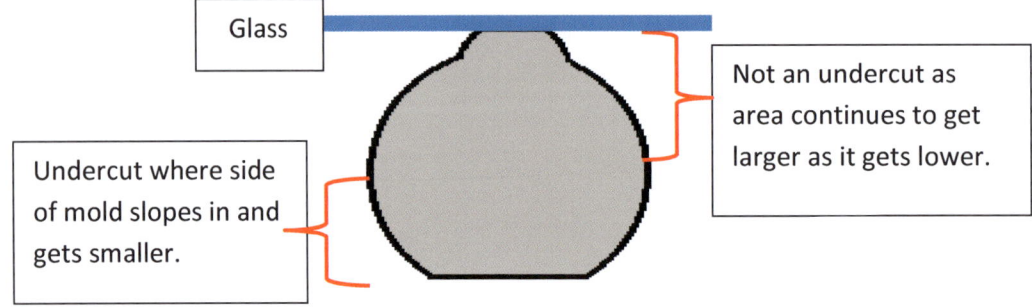

c. Glass is over-slumped

An example of an overslumped piece is where the glass was cut a bit larger than the mold circumference. Generally speaking, the glass size should not exceed about ¼" more than the outside edge of the mold or the fuser will risk over-slumping. In this case, the edges of glass curl around the edge of the mold and make the glass stick.

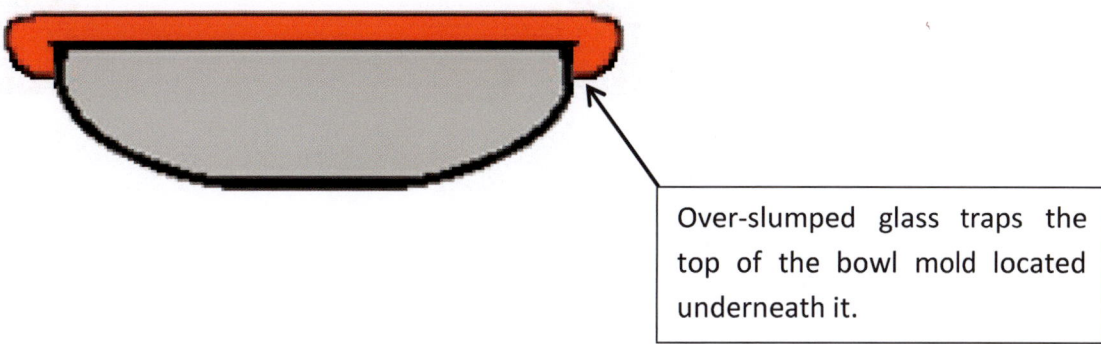

Over-slumped glass traps the top of the bowl mold located underneath it.

If a glass piece has become pinched by a mold due to over slumping or small undercuts, it is *sometimes* possible to remove the glass from the mold without breaking it. This is only possible if the mold has been coated with release agent on the outside as well as the inside. In this case, the mold with attached glass should be placed upside down (mold side up) in the kiln and reheated to about 1000°F. At this point, you may be able to reach in and remove the mold from the glass. Re-anneal the glass and return it to room temperature slowly. Be sure to wear adequate heat protection and eye protection if you plan to do this! Also, plan ahead where you will put the hot mold once removed. On top of the kiln is a good place as it is handy and it can withstand the heat. (You may need a second person to help you in this process.)

d. Distortions caused by steep sided molds.

It is difficult to slump accurately and symmetrically down a steep-sided mold. Glass tends to slump in a lopsided way and may end up as an uneven puddle at the bottom of the mold.

Solutions:

One way to prevent this occurrence is to use a series of molds from shallow to middle to deep, each with the same (if a lip exists), or progressively slightly smaller, diameter at the opening. Such multi-molds are available from glass stores or you can try to assemble your own from stainless steel bowls found at a thrift store.

| Step 1 | Step 2 | Step 3 |

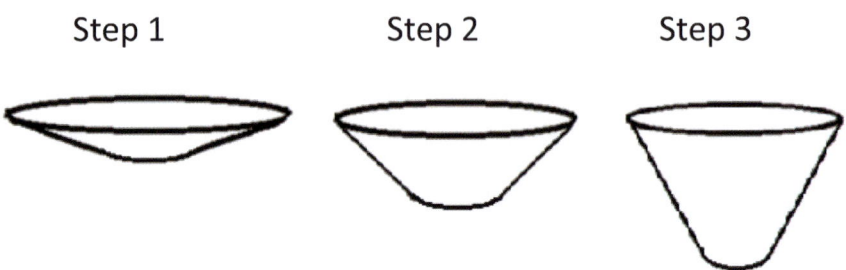

A second way to make a reasonably deep dish is to drape it over the back of a stainless steel bowl. The result will not be as deep as the 3-mold process, however. The glossy surface will necessarily be on the outside of the bowl in this case. Care must be taken to avoid using a flat piece which is much larger than the bowl, as draping this may cause fluting at the usual draping temperature of 1200°F. To minimize fluting and create a slightly deeper result, try taking the kiln temperature up a little bit higher to 1205-1210°F or so, but be careful that the glass doesn't slip down too far on the mold and create an undercut or a glob on the shelf!

Glass   Mold

If fluting is not problematic, then the piece can be draped over any suitable vase or bowl mold.

The best way to make a deep vessel is by dropping it through a donut mold followed by removing the rim. (See Chapter 17)

e. Fall through from the drop out mold.

A common problem when attempting to drop glass though a hole in a drop-out mold is finding that the glass has slipped all the way through the hole onto the kiln shelf.

Prevent this problem in the future by using a slower ramp up in temperature (no faster than 300°F/hour) and by stopping the ramp at a lower top temperature (no hotter than 1330°F).

****

Chapter 9: Using Refractories

Hot glass sticks to anything, just the way hot sugar does. Of course, hot sugar only ventures into the 300 degrees Fahrenheit range but still can produce a fatal burn. Glass fusing temperatures are said to be in the "warm" glass range of 1400 to 1700 degrees, whereas glass blowing is done near the top range of 2300 degrees. The point here is that hot or warm, it will burn you, and when it does, it will stick to you. So, be careful!

Because "warm" and hot glasses stick to anything, you will need to put some kind of refractory substance between the glass and the kiln shelf or the mold to prevent sticking. Refractories are usually either liquid, powder to which you add a liquid like water, or some kind of fibrous material.

Some refractory always remains on the glass after fusing, therefore, care must be taken to remove this refractory residue, regardless of the type, before the back side of the glass can be re-fused onto another piece of glass.

1. Kiln Washes

Two main types of kiln washes are available today: High fire and Primo primer. High fire is great when used for multiple firings and is used to paint the new kiln bottom and ceramic molds. Kiln shelves need frequent resurfacing with refractory agents, however.

Because of this, Primo primer was developed. High fire release requires scraping and sanding to remove it before reapplication and the next firing. Primo primer, though, is easily washed off with a rag and water. Primo only lasts for one or two firings, whereas High Fire primer lasts through several. They both work. The choice is yours.

High fire kiln wash is the most commonly used refractory in fusing. It is a mix of minerals which have been finely ground. It comes in a powder form to which you add water. Be sure to coat the floor of your brand new kiln with a high fire kiln wash before you ever use it. This will ensure that any glass which falls off a shelf won't stick to the kiln and destroy the fire bricks. Take care not to inhale the powder of refractory kiln wash by wearing a painter's mask when mixing up a batch.

Next, each shelf must be coated with kiln wash. Paint several thin coats of wash on the shelf until it is more purple or pink than shelf colored. Follow the directions on the label to cure the wash before fusing your glass. With some types all you need to do is wait for it to air dry. Other types require you to heat it in the kiln before using it. The shelf will need to be sanded or scraped free of wash after use. If you fail to replace the wash with new wash before a fusing, you run the risk of the wash sticking to the back of your piece and being extremely difficult to remove. Because scraping off the old shelf wash was a pain before the development of Primo, I sometimes risked fusing two or three times before cleaning off my shelf and starting again. Occasionally, I was sorry I did this.

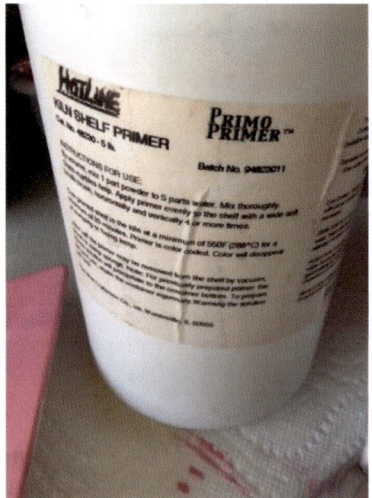

I find kiln wash mixes more easily when I add the powder to the bowl first and then add the water. I mix it with an old whisk or a spoon. Only mix what you need as it dries up in a few days. Coat the entire surface that glass will touch to prevent adhesion.

A third type of wash is meant for stainless steel molds. Boron nitride spray is a wonderful addition to the refractories collection. It is simply sprayed onto the stainless steel mold surface and can easily be reapplied. Several brands are available. Like shelf paper, however, it has temperature limitations. Read the directions on the can carefully.

2. Refractory Kiln Shelf Covers

Refractory kiln paper and kiln blanket materials are readily available online and at art glass stores. These surfaces will only last through one high temperature or possibly two low temperature firings, but are easy to replace. Just cut out a piece big enough to protect your glass completely from touching the kiln shelf and place your art on top of it before firing. The back side of your glass piece will not be as smooth as if you placed it directly onto the shelf surface, however.

 Thin kiln blanket

Textured kiln cloth (Lava cloth) is another refractory sheet material which can be placed under your art glass. There are several styles available. It leaves a nice pattern in the glass. If you use it, your glass will retain the pattern even if you change your mind and try to smooth it out again later, however.

Kiln cloth will add texture to the back of a piece to provide interest.

****

Chapter 10: Basic Fusing Techniques

1. Tack Fusing

Tack fusing employs the minimum amount of heat to make one glass stick to another glass. Tack fused glass has rounded edges, is fully polished and provides texture to a piece of art glass.

    a. Equipment for Tack Fusing
    You will need at least two separate pieces of compatible glass and a prepared kiln with a tack fusing program.

    b. Process of Tack Fusing
        1) Place the second pieces(s) of glass onto the base glass in your selected design.
        2) Fuse the glasses to about 1400 degrees Fahrenheit.

    c. Kiln Program for Tack Fusing

(This is an example for two to three medium sized layers only. The actual ramp speeds and hold times will depend upon how big and thick your glass design is. Bigger and/or thicker means you need to go slower and hold longer.)

Ramp 1: 300 degrees/hour up to 1000 degrees
Ramp 2: 1500 degrees/hour up to **1400** degrees
Ramp 3: 9999 degrees/hour (As Fast As Possible) down to 1000 degrees
Ramp 4: 150 degrees/hour down to 900 degrees
Hold: 1 hour and 25 minutes (1:25) or longer
Ramp 5: 300 degrees/hour down to 300 degrees

Program is complete.

Wait to open the kiln until it is room temperature or no more than 150 degrees.

d. Pitfalls of Tack Fusing
1) Poor color or design choices
2) Incompatible glass
3) Not enough heat
4) Raising temperature too fast
5) Too little annealing
6) Opening the kiln too soon

e. Results

The best tack fusing technique results in a piece with distinct edges on the superimposed upper glass.

This piece was inspired by something I saw on the Delphi glass gallery website. It was so beautiful; I couldn't resist making something similar.

2. Full Fusing

a. Equipment for Full Fusing

The equipment for full fusing is the same as for tack fusing, but the kiln program differs.

b. Process of Full Fusing

1) Place the second pieces(s) of glass onto the base glass in your selected design.
2) Fuse the glass pieces to about 1500 degrees Fahrenheit.

c. Kiln Program for Full Fusing

Ramp 1: 300 degrees/hour up to 1000 degrees
Ramp 2: 1500 degrees/hour up to **1500** degrees
Ramp 3: 9999 degrees/hour (As Fast As Possible) down to 1000 degrees
Ramp 4: 150 degrees/hour down to 900 degrees
Hold: 1 hour and 25 minutes (1:25) or longer
Ramp 5: 300 degrees/hour down to 300 degrees
Program is complete.
Wait to open the kiln until it is room temperature or no more than 150 degrees.

d. Pitfalls of Full Fusing

1) Poor color or design choices
2) Incompatible glass
3) Not enough heat

4) Raising temperature too fast
5) Too little annealing
6) Opening the kiln too soon
7) Unwanted bubbles

e. Results

The best full fusing technique results in a piece with no distinct edges on the superimposed, upper glass. The glass will appear flat and smooth.

3. Slumping into a Mold

a. Equipment for Slumping
1) A piece of glass, previously fused or not,
2) Prepared mold
3) A prepared kiln with a slumping program

b. Process of Slumping
1) Make sure the mold has been prepared with a release agent.

2) Be sure the glass is no more than 1/8" larger than the edge of the mold.
3) Place the glass on the mold.
4) Place in kiln and close the lid.
5) Set kiln for slumping program with a high point somewhere around 1200 to 1300 degrees Fahrenheit.
6) Press start.
7) Wait.

c. Kiln Program for Slumping

Ramp 1: 300 degrees/hour up to 1250 degrees

Ramp 2: 9999 degrees/hour (As Fast As Possible) down to 1000 degrees

Ramp 3: 150 degrees/hour down to 900 degrees

Hold: 1hour and 25 minutes (1:25) or longer

Ramp 4: 300 degrees/hour down to 300 degrees

Program is complete.

Wait to open the kiln until it is room temperature or no more than 150 degrees.

d. Pitfalls of Slumping
1) Not hot enough
2) Too hot and too slow causing devitrification
3) Same pitfalls as in tack and full fusing programs

e. Results
The best slumping results reveal the shape of the mold.

4. Draping Over a Mold

a. Equipment for Draping
   1) A piece of glass
   2) A stainless steel mold which has been prepared with mold release agent (Do not use aluminum as it will melt in the kiln.)
   3) A small circle of fiber blanket on top of the inverted mold to cover where the glass will rest
   4) A prepared kiln with a draping program readied

b. Process of Draping

  1) Place the draping mold in the kiln.

  2) Place your glass piece on top of the mold being sure that the glass touches only the fiber blanket.

  3) Close the kiln.

  4) Set the kiln program for a draping cycle.

  5) Press start.

  6) Wait.

c. Kiln Program for Draping:

  Ramp 1: 300°F/hour up to **1200°F**

Ramp 2: 1000°F/hour down to 1000°

Ramp 3: 150°F/hour down to 900°F

Hold at 900°F for 1 ½ hours

Ramp 4: 200°F/hour down to 300°F

Program is complete.

Do not open the kiln until it reaches 150°F or below.

d. Pitfalls in Draping

a. Failure to use thermal cushion on top of mold causes glass to crack or break when heated.
b. Kiln program is too hot and glass slides down too far on mold.
c. Kiln program is too hot and glass gets trapped on mold in undercuts (where mold is narrower after first being wider)

Undercuts make it difficult or impossible to remove the glass from the mold.

e. Results

The best full fusing technique results in a piece with no distinct edges on the superimposed, upper glass. The glass will appear flat and smooth.

The "handkerchief" vase is a prime example of a draped piece.

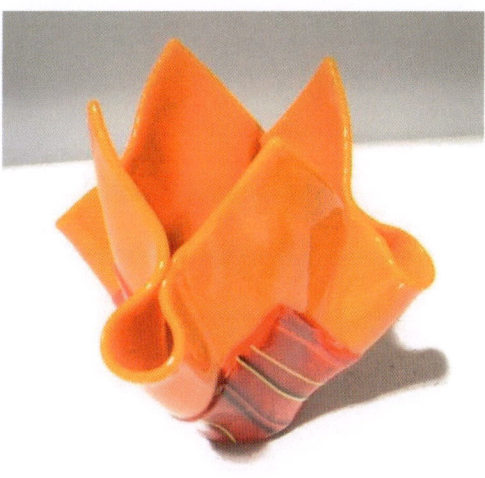

****

"We have had a long love affair with glass. It inspires us with its beauty, surprises us with its versatility, challenges us with its complex physical properties, and transforms our lives with its unique technical capabilities."

Wendell Weeks, Chairman, Chief Executive Officer and President, Corning Incorporated

Chapter 11: Fixing Unwanted Bubbles

1. Equipment

    a. The equipment needed to repair unwanted bubbles depends upon the size of the bubbles.

    b. Glass cutting or grinding tools

    c. Kiln

2. Processes of fixing unwanted bubbles

    a. Prevent the bubbles from forming in the first place by soaking the glass:

Many people do what they call a "soak" or "hold" temperature during fusing. There are times when it is a definite must. First, if the glass is not absolutely flat, air can be trapped between layers when you fuse them together. This can create undesirable bubbles. Much glass is textured and therefore, is not perfectly flat. To prevent most of this trapped air, soaking the glass during the heating phase at around 1200°F - 1250° F for a half hour or so will often flatten it such that minimal air will be trapped when the glass reaches fusing temperature. When fusing small pieces of glass to a bigger piece, air can usually escape out the edges, which makes this low temperature soak unneeded during the heat phase.

    b. Large bubble fixes.

Occasionally, even the practiced artist will find bubbles in the fused piece. In this case, a very large bubble was inadvertently formed during heating.

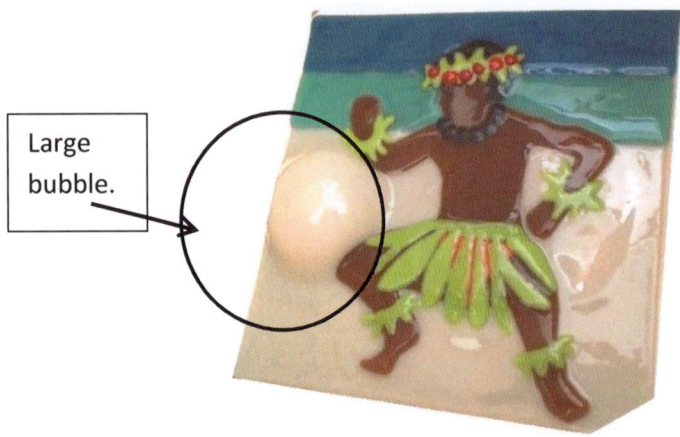

Large bubble.

This huge bubble ruins an otherwise nice plate of a Hawaiian dancer on the beach. What happened? Here, the sand-colored piece was a single layer while the rest of the plate was two or more layers. During a tack fuse program, the single layer heated faster and hotter than the multi-layered areas. As the glass changed shape unequally during heating, a bit of air was trapped underneath the piece causing the single layer region to bubble up. The piece was saved, fortunately. Here is what I did:

First, the plate was reheated slowly (300 °F per hour) just enough to flatten it out without causing the bubble to rupture, to 1250 degrees.

A very thin layer of glass remains.

Next, glass leaves of a ti plant were added over the thin region.

The plate was fused one more time to 1405°F. Each fusing further flattened the plate removing almost all of its texture, but it is still quite attractive nonetheless.

c. Medium sized bubble fixes:

In this second example, a somewhat smaller bubble was formed as air was trapped between glass layers.

The solution for this unplanned bubble was to incorporate it into the design. In this plate, I made the bubble into a cloud by painting the circumference with a gold pen.

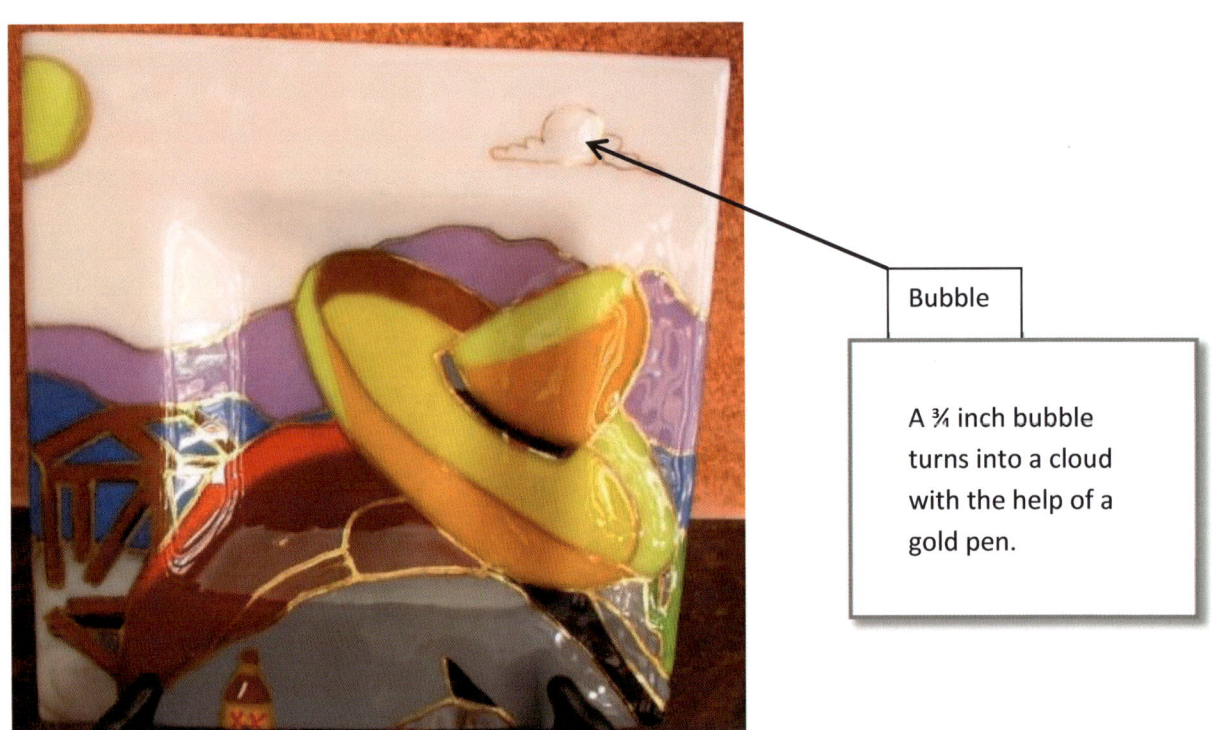

Bubble

A ¾ inch bubble turns into a cloud with the help of a gold pen.

d. Very small bubbles:

A common issue is the development of many small bubbles after fusing large pieces together as seen between the neo-lavender layers here.

There are a few approaches to minimizing this type of bubbling.

1) Decide that it looks nice as is and adds some sparkle to your piece.

2) Use smaller pieces on top of a single large layer. Air can usually escape easily from small pieces which avoids most bubbles.

3) Soak the piece at 1250 degrees for a half hour or more to flatten the layers as much as possible before they are fused together.

e. Repairing large popped bubbles:

In the instance where a large bubble actually ruptures, the area first must be flattened as described above. The temperature must be raised very slowly to minimize enlargement of the hole.

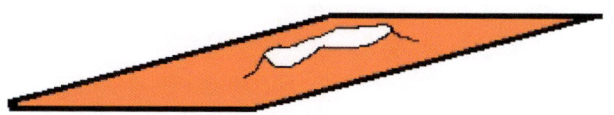

Next, cut a piece of replacement glass to put inside the hole. To do this, make a pattern for your glass by tracing the hole's shape on a piece of paper placed under the hole. Stick the paper pattern onto the replacement glass and cut around the edges.

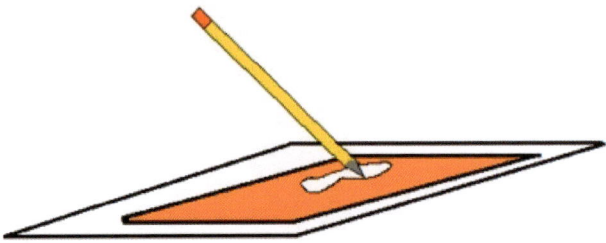

Place the glass in the hole.

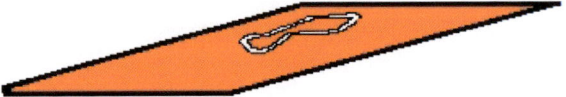

At this point, place a sheet of clear under the entire piece and full fuse it again. If you want to use similar glass, place the sheet above rather than under the original layer.

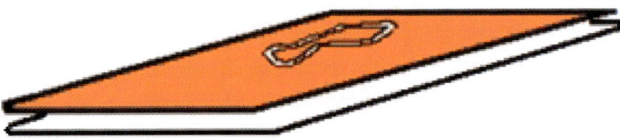

3. Kiln Programs

a. The exact programs used will vary depending on what you are trying to accomplish, but suffice it to say a tack fusing program will stick things together and a full fusing program will meld them seamlessly.

4. Pitfalls in Repairing Unwanted Bubbles

a. The only real pitfall is failure to repair the problem adequately.
b. At times like these, as you toss the glass in the waste can, it is wise to remember that nothing ventured is nothing gained. At worst, you learned what *not* to do.

5. Results

Bubbles gone is the best outcome possible.

****

"Double, double toil and trouble; Fire burn, and caldron bubble."

'Macbeth' by William Shakespeare

Part II: Adding Cold Work to Fusing Techniques

Chapter 12: Screen Melting

Both screen melting and pot melting are good ways to convert glass scraps into art objects.

1. Equipment for Screen melting:

a. Stainless steel screen with roughly ½" squares – NOT prepared with mold primer

b. Stainless steel ring or open-bottomed square stainless steel pan 2"- 4" tall

c. Fiber blanket cut and fitted around insides of pan.

d. Glass scraps – about 3 lbs. for 15" diameter ring pan but amount depends on the size of the ring or square

e. Shelf in kiln prepared with shelf primer or fiber blanket

f. 4 Kiln posts about 3" tall if pan sides are less than 2" high

2. Screen Melting Process

A useful way to use glass scraps is screen melting or pot melting. Screen melting and Pot melting are similar processes. Both involve melting glass from above and letting it drip into a mold clad inside with fiber paper or blanket.

NOTE: A third process which lets molten glass drip from a hole in the bottom of the kiln and is then manipulated outside the kiln is vitrigraph fusing. It requires a special kiln and is not included in this text.

The difference between the pot melt and the screen melt is how the dripping occurs. In the screen melt process, the glass drips from where it sits on the screen. With pot melting, the drips pour through the holes in the bottom of the pot.

Ready for the melt. Note: Mainly light colors are used and they are mostly kept separate from each other to minimize color muddying.

Small drips form circles which meld together.

a. Cover the inside of the ring or square with fiber blanket and set on a primered or fiber-blanketed shelf.

b. Cut a stainless steel circle from the screen. Do NOT use shelf primer on the screen.

c. Place about 3 pounds of glass scraps on top of the screen.

(Note: placing similar glass colors next to each other produces a generally better effect than mixing all the colors randomly. Random colors often result in a muddy looking product.)

d. Fuse at 1650 degrees F. without a Hold, or optionally, 1550 degrees with a Hold of 45 minutes.

    (Note: See Kiln Program for details.)

e. Remove glass from kiln when cool, trim edges, and fire polish as needed.

    (Note: the glass piece will be nearly ¼ inch thick and difficult to cut without a ring saw, tile saw or some other type of electric wet saw.)

3. Kiln program for Screen Melting:

    Ramp 1: 500 degrees/hr. up to1000 degrees

    Ramp 2: 1500 degrees/hr. up to 1650 degrees

    Ramp 3: 9999 degrees/hr. down to 1000 degrees

    Ramp 4: 150 degrees/hr. down to 900 degrees

    Hold at 900 degrees for 1hr. and 45 minutes

    Ramp 5: 300 degrees/hr. down to 300 degrees

    Program is complete. Let glass rest until kiln is 150 degrees or below. Only then, open the kiln.

4. Pitfalls of Screen Melting and Pot Melting:

a. The glass doesn't all flow through to the shelf.
Obviously, this happens when the glass is not hot enough. It is important to remember that the change in temperature of the glass is usually slower than the kiln by about 50 degrees. Therefore, as the kiln just reaches 1650 degrees, the glass may only be 1600 degrees. A hold may be needed.

Screen melted glass which hasn't quite all dripped through may form small apparent stalagmites on the surface of the glass as seen here:

These interesting-looking protrusions are easily broken off and generally disappear when the piece is fire polished. If a lapidary disc is available, the glass surface can be smoothed with a gentle grinding before the fire polishing.

b. Spalling.
Spalling is something that often happens to the stainless steel ring. Bits of steel flake off during cooling. These black flakes can make the artist think the piece is ruined. Usually, however, the flakes fall off as

soon as the piece of glass is removed from the steel mold and the glass is unharmed.

If a used steel mold causes spalling during the rise in temperature, the black flakes will become imbedded in the glass creating small to large black areas which will often ruin the piece. This may happen if the steel has not been cleaned of flakes from a previous firing. Care should be taken to clean the steel ring as well as possible and then cover the entire inside of the steel mold with fiber blanket to minimize the chance of spalling.

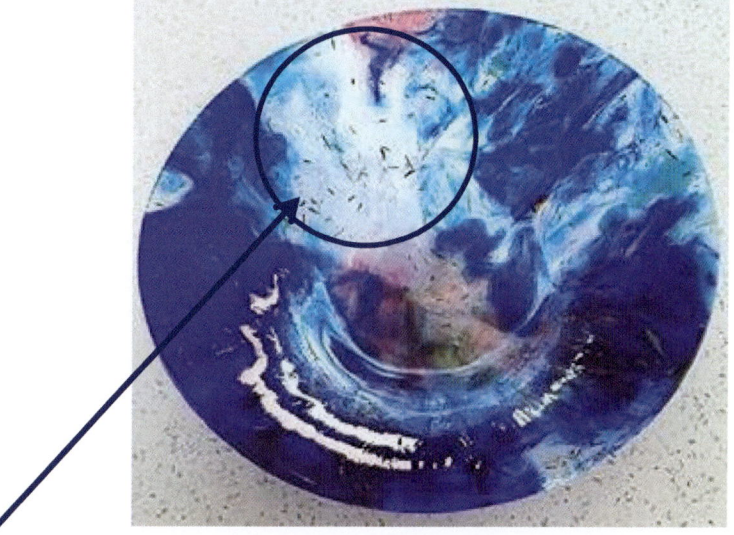

Tiny bits of spalling can be seen in the picture between 11 and 12 o'clock.

Nonetheless, the screen-melted bowl is a success.

c. The colors look dark and muddied after melting.

This may happen when too many different colored glass scraps are mixed randomly. The best way to add different colors is to make collections of each color on the screen or in the pot. They can certainly overlap, but the majority of each color should be distinct from the next one.

Screen melted bowl with dark, muddied areas.

5. Results

Pieces of a failed vase were screen melted, and new pieces were added to the edge to make this bowl. A few scraps can go a long way.

* *

"A singer can shatter *glass* with the proper high note," he said, "but the simplest way to break *glass* is simply to drop it on the floor. "

Anne Rice, author

Chapter 13: Pot Melting

Pot melted glass tends to drip into a pond-like pattern with a rippling colors effect. The overall effect of pot melting is quite different from screen melting, but both are unique and lovely.

1. Equipment for Pot melting:

   a. Crucible or a Clay flower pot with hole(s) in the bottom – Do NOT paint with primer. Note: Additional holes may be drilled in the bottom of the pot using a drill and bit for glass or ceramics if desired.

   b. Ring or open-bottomed square stainless steel pan
   c. Fiber blanket cut into strips and fitted around insides of pan
   d. Glass scraps – about 3 lbs. for 15" diameter pan. The amount depends on the size of the ring or square
   e. Shelf in kiln prepared with shelf primer or fiber blanket
   f. Kiln posts long enough to span the diameter of the ring or square.

2. Pot Melting Process:

   a. Set up the pot as shown below. Do not coat the pot or crucible with shelf primer as this may become incorporated in the glass and ruin the effect. Be sure to place strips of fiber blanket around the inside of the ring or square and fiber blanket or shelf primer on the shelf to prevent melted glass from sticking. Do not coat the inside of the pot or crucible with shelf primer or fiber blanket. (See Chapter 22.)

Prepared for Pot Melt

Note that the posts which span the ring do not obstruct the bottom hole in the pot. Only one color of glass was used here.

   b. Fuse.

3. Kiln Program for Pot Melting

Ramp 1: 500 degrees/hr. up to1000 degrees

Ramp 2: 1500 degrees/hr. up to 1650 degrees

Hold: for 30 minutes.

Ramp 3: 9999 degrees/hr. down to 1000 degrees

Ramp 4: 150 degrees/hr. down to 900 degrees

Hold at 900 degrees for 1hr. and 45 minutes or longer.

Ramp 5: 300 degrees/hr. down to 300 degrees

Program is complete. Let glass rest until kiln is 150 degrees or below.

Only then, open the kiln.

4. Pitfalls

The pitfalls for pot melts are essentially the same as for screen melts.

5. Results

After the pot melt

Before slumping

After slumping

****

Chapter 14: Pattern Bars

Pattern bars are relatively easy for the beginner to make. Interesting and complex looking art pieces can result.

1. Equipment for Pattern Bars
    a. 6 or more layers of glass strips
    b. Fiber blanket strips the same size
    c. Fiber blanket covering the kiln shelf
    d. Fire bricks
    e. A good wet tile saw or similar is needed to cut them into little slices.

2. Process of Making Pattern Bars

Pattern bars are made by cutting strips of glass, stacking then, fusing them together and then slicing them into small squares. The squares are then arranged onto a piece of background glass in differing design patterns.

    a. Cut strips of differing glasses and stack them.

b. Place on fiber blanketed kiln shelf.

c. Place fiber blanket on ends and sides of glass stack and push together with fire bricks until stack is supported on 4 sides.

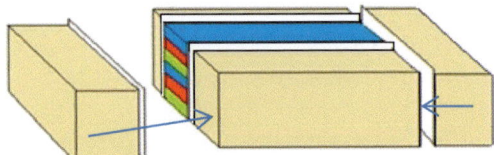

d. Fuse and allow bar to cool before removing from kiln.

e. Trim and slice bar using wet saw.

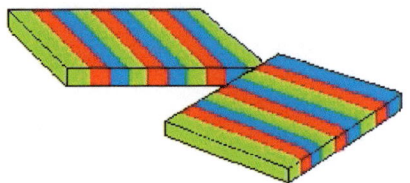

f. Arrange on background glass into pleasing design.

g. Fuse again and slump as desired.

3. Pattern Bar Kiln Program

Ramp 1: 300 degrees/hour up to 1000 degrees
Hold for 20 minutes
Ramp 2: 1500 degrees/hour up to 1500 degrees

Ramp 3: 9999 degrees/hour down to 1000 degrees

Ramp 4: 150 degrees/hour down to 900 degrees

Hold for 2 hours or longer depending on number of layers

Ramp 5: 200 degrees/hours down to 300 degrees

Program is complete but wait to open the kiln until temperature is 150 degrees or lower

4. Pitfalls

There are relatively few pitfalls to pattern bar making. If less than a full fuse is used, the layers may separate during slicing. Similarly, if the saw blade is dull or not fine enough, pieces of the glass may chip during cutting.

5. Results

This tweed design was made of three different pattern bars.

****

Chapter 15: Flow-Through Bars

Making flow-through bars is similar to making pattern bars in that glass is stacked up in a pile and fused together. The bars are sliced and arranged on background piece of glass too. The difference comes both in how the glass is fused and how the slices are arranged after.

1. Equipment for Flow-Through Bars

a. 4 Kiln fire bricks

b. Stack of at least 8 pieces of glass in varying colors about a half inch shorter than the firebricks

c. Fiber blanket or a thick layer of kiln wash to cover bricks and prevent glass sticking

d. 2 or 3 Stainless steel rods about 3/16 inches in diameter and about 8 inches long

2. Flow-Through Bar Process

a. Cut and stack the strips of glass.

b. Drill two ½ inch holes in each end of the firebrick as high as possible. (An alternate method is to use a stainless steel loaf pan and drill holes in each end just below the rim.)

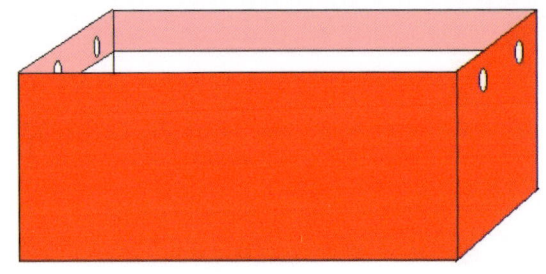

c. If using fire bricks, arrange them to make a small rectangle on the fiber blanketed kiln shelf.

d. Cover the sides of the loaf pan with fiber blanket up to the holes.

e. Place the rods through the holes. Do not paint them with shelf primer.

f. Place strips of glass on top of the rods.

g. Fire to a full fuse. Remember that your glass is six or more layers thick and will need a slow program and a long annealing time.

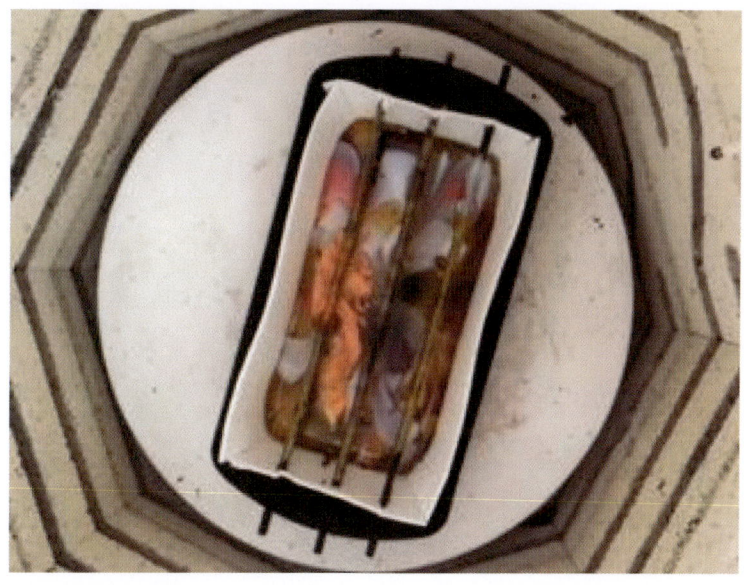

h. After fusing, remove the glass brick from the pan.

i. Clean up the bricks before slicing them with a wet saw.

j. Thinly slice the solid brick with a wet saw for tiles. Retrieve each slice after it is cut to be sure the slices are kept in sequence.

k. Arrange the slices in a pleasing pattern on a base glass. Often, a butterfly pattern is chosen wherein two slices cut next to each other are splayed open. Butterflying is shown below.

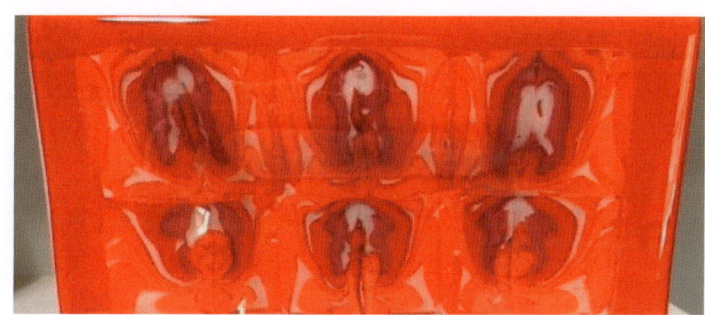

l. Full fuse again. (The glass is now much thinner and will not need such a long annealing time or slow processing.)

3. Flow-Through Bar Kiln Program

Ramp 1: 300 degrees F/hour up to 1000 degrees

Hold: 30 minutes

Ramp 2: 1500 degrees/hour up to 1550 degrees

Hold: 20 minutes

Ramp 3: 9999 degrees/hour down to 1000 degrees

Ramp 4: 150 degrees/hour down to 900 degrees

Hold: 2 hours or more depending on thickness of layered slab of glass

Ramp 5: 300 degrees/hour down to 300 degrees

Wait to open kiln until temperature is 150 degrees or below.

4. Flow-Through Bar Pitfalls

a. Glass fails to fall all the way through the rods to the bottom.
    Obviously, the fuser needs either more heat or a longer hold time.
    Fortunately, the whole kit and caboodle can be re-fused to get the
    remaining glass down into the bar.

b. Glass is stuck to the firebrick.
    Prevent this with either a very thick layer of kiln shelf primer or with a
    fiber blanket liner on the mold sides.

c. Losing sequence of the slices.
    This can make splaying the slices open like butterflies or a Rorschach ink
    blot difficult if not impossible. Prevent this by retrieving each slice as it is
    cut and stacking them in sequence.

5. Results

It is important to keep the slices in order so that you can butterfly them
open for best effect when placing them on a background piece of glass.
In the following picture it is easy to see how the slices were butterflied
open to create the design.

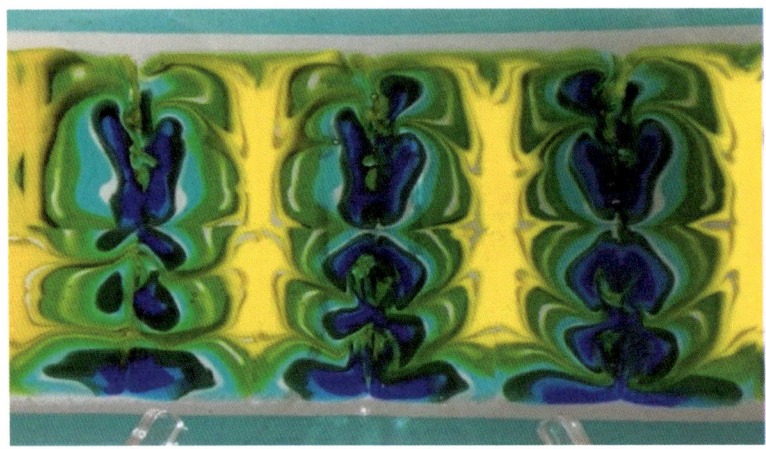

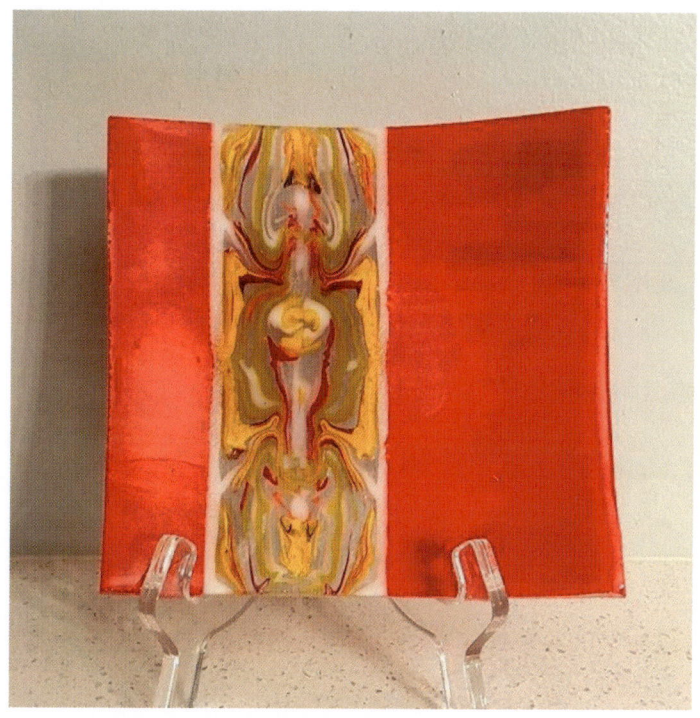

The seemingly intricate flow-through bar above was easily made from a leftover ring removed from a vase previously made by the artist. Scrap glass can often be reused several times.

The group of flow-through bars on the left was made from the ring of scrap glass after cutting the top off of this vase shown on the right. Scraps are art!

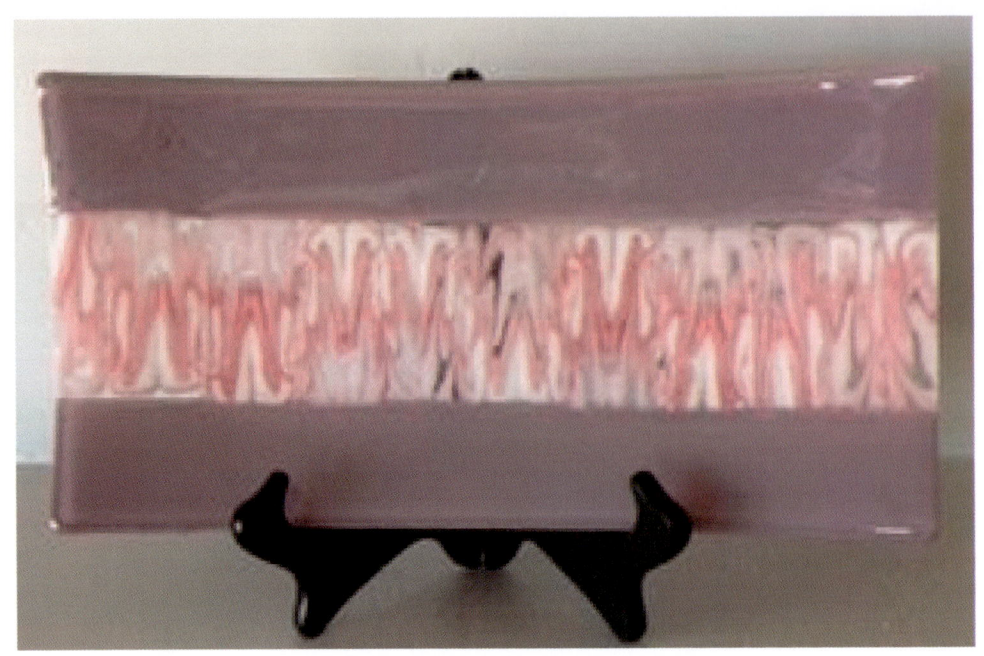

Typical flow-through plate

Squares from a flow through bar were alternated with orange squares and the whole piece was placed on a clear background which was cut away around the top squares to make this design.

****

Chapter 16: Making Glass Boxes

Blueberries

Glass boxes make lovely little presents. When they are handmade, they are incomparable and sure to be treasured by the recipient. Making a single box takes several days, but when it is finished, the artist has something to be proud of.

1. Equipment for Making Glass Boxes
    a. Clear glass for all background pieces
    b. Colored glass (compatible with clear) for all decorations
    c. Clear Gorilla Glue or silicone glue (It is important that it is *clear*!)
    d. Wax paper
    e. Sticky tape such as Scotch tape
    f. One roughly 6 inch by 3" piece of wood with **right angles**
    g. Patience. Making boxes takes time, but it is definitely worth it.

2. Process of Making Glass Boxes

The process of making glass boxes uses both fusing and glue because I haven't been able to figure out how to fuse the whole box and stick the sides together without it. All the sides need to be fused first at about 1400 degrees F to round off their edges and fuse the decorations on after which, the cooled sides are glued together. I use a piece of wood with 90 degree sides as a jig to hold things square while the glue dries. But take care that the glue doesn't stick permanently to the wood and glass simultaneously, or your box will be in deep trouble. Wax paper helps to prevent the wood from sticking, but it can become stuck itself.

a. Cut two sides of clear glass as nearly the same as possible. Make each about 6 inches by 3 inches. These will become the long sides of the box.

b. Cut 2 equal end pieces for the short sides which are 3 inches by 3 inches. (Obviously, this is only an example, and you can make your box any size you want.)

c. Cut 2 more pieces for the top and bottom. Make these pieces ¼ inch bigger in both length and width than the side and end pieces (i.e. 6 ¼ inches by 3 ¼ inches).

d. Cut one slightly smaller piece of clear glass 2 ½ inches by 5 ½ inches. This piece will eventually be glued to the underside of the lid to keep it from sliding off the box.

e. Decorate top, sides and ends with whatever design you have in mind.

f. Either tack fuse or full fuse all pieces as desired, but keep in mind that tack fusing will distort the size of the sides less than full fusing and make it easier to join the sides.

g. Cover the wood block with wax paper and tape completely.

h. Place the bottom and one long side against the block as shown below:

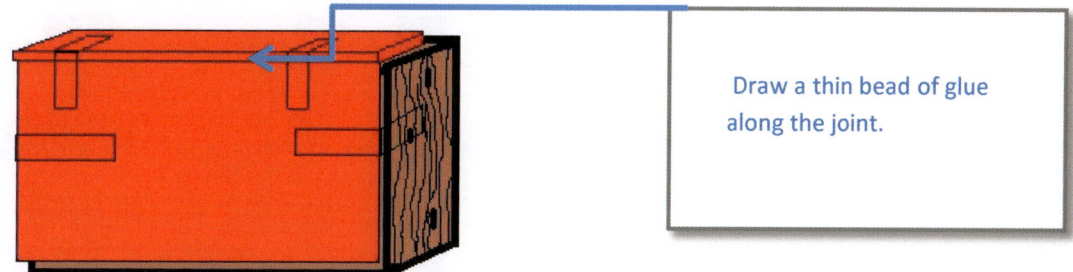

Draw a thin bead of glue along the joint.

i. Tape the glass bottom and one side piece to the wax-papered wood block.

j. Glue the side to the bottom along the joint and allow to dry overnight.

k. Remove the wax paper-covered wood and sticky tape when dry.

l. Add one end piece of glass and attach to the first two glass pieces with sticky tape. Re-cover wood with wax paper. Glue another bead along each of the two new joints. Allow to dry overnight. The box now has 3 sides.

m. Re-cover the wood with waxed paper, turn it on its end and fit it into the three-sided box to provide support to the end piece. The box is now 4-sided.

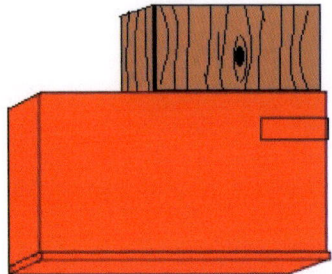

Four-sided box has a bottom and three sides.

n. Join the fifth side to the bottom and the other three sides to make a five-sided box. Glue thin beads along each of the new joints. The wood is no longer needed. Tape and the supporting four sides will be enough to hold the box together.

o. Place four small spots of glue to the underside of the box lid to join the box lid with the smaller piece of glass which will prevent the lid from sliding off the box. Allow to dry.

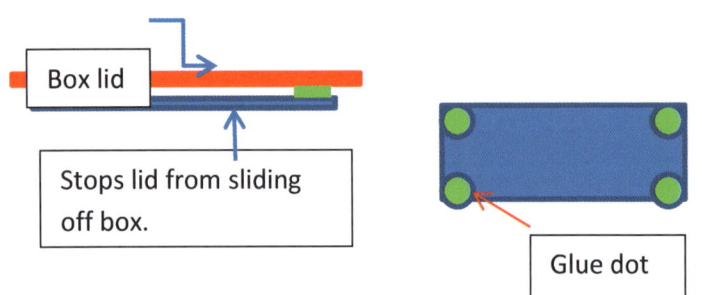

Box lid

Stops lid from sliding off box.

Glue dot

A dot of clear glue is added to corners of the small lid cover which is then adhered to the underside of the box top.

Your box is finished and will hold trinkets for years to come if it doesn't fall on the floor!

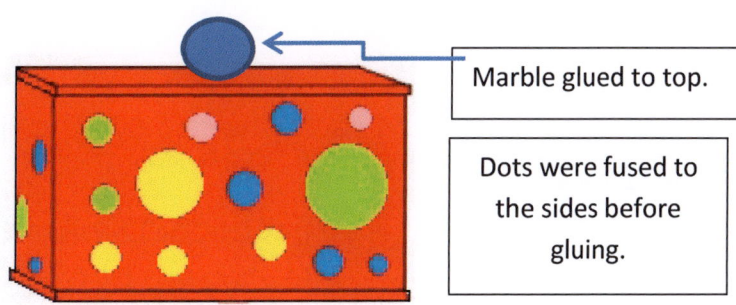

Marble glued to top.

Dots were fused to the sides before gluing.

3. Kiln Programs for Making Glass Boxes
    a. Tack fusing program can be:

    Ramp 1: 500 degrees F per hour up to 100 degrees F.

    Ramp 2: 1500 degrees F per hour up to 1400 degrees F.

    Ramp 3: Cool at 9999 degrees F per hour down to 1000 degrees F.

    Ramp 4: 150 degrees F per hour down to 900 degrees

    Hold for 1 hour at 900 degrees.

    Ramp 5: 300 degrees per hour down to 400 degrees F.

    Program is Complete. Wait to open kiln until 150 degrees F or lower.

b. For a full fusing program, use the same as above but stop Ramp 2 at 1480 – 1500 degrees.

4. Pitfalls

A few unfortunate things can happen when making glass boxes. Most can be prevented or remedied, however.

a. Pieces are not cut eactly the same side to side, end to end, and top to bottom.
This means it may be difficult or impossible to set the sides onto the bottom squarely and box angles will not end up square. If you want your box to look symmetrical and square, you may need to recut the offending piece.

b. Wax paper sticks to the glass.
Prevent this by removing the wax paper as needed from under joints before it is completely dry. Take care, however, to be sure the wet glue doesn't stick to the wood support. The wood needs to be left in place until the joint is completely dry.

c. The glued joints look yellow.
It is a must that the glue looks absolutely colorless and clear in the bottle before you use it as it *will* show at the joints. Take care when buying Gorilla Glue as it comes in opaque, a nearly clear yellow, and completely clear forms. You must use the completely clear variety to avoid having it show at the joint lines. Clear Gorilla Glue is readily available at big box hardware stores and other stores and does a good job on glass without showing. A tube of E-6000 or clear silicone work well also.

d. Glue gets onto the glass where you don't want it.

Sometimes you can remedy this if the glue has not set for too long by taking a paint scraper or putty knife to it the scrape it off.

5. Results.

I have included examples of finished boxes as springboards for your own ideas:

Cherries from flowers to fruit.

Pond Life

A mold for a lotus flower was used to produce the three-dimensional flower shown here. It is a 3-piece mold available online. After fusing all three pieces separately, they were glued together and then glued to the box top. The frogs were drawn freehand as a paper pattern and cut with a Taurus ring saw before fusing.

* * * * * * * * * * * * * * * * *

Chapter 17: Glass Tapestry

Glass tapestry is relatively easy to make but looks complicated and lovely. The designs within "rugs" of glass can be quite simple, or can look highly complex with circles within circles on real fabric. Although it takes a lot of stringers to make a piece, the results can be stunning.

1. Equipment for Making Glass Tapestry
   a. Stringers of multiple colors
   b. Clear glass for background – 2 pieces
   c. Wet saw

2. Process of Making Glass Tapestry
   a. Place parallel stringers onto clear background sheet of glass in the color sequence of your choice. Make sure they do not overlap.

Random colored stringers on clear background.

b. Tack fuse

c. Turn glass 90 degrees and cut ½ inch slices while keeping slices in their original sequence.

d. Place strips on a new background piece of clear glass.

e. While keeping the slices flat on the table, push some of them up or down to create a wave-like pattern. Note: if you combine patterns by alternating slices from two or more separate fused stringer sheets, the designs can become more complex.

e. Cut off each strip along the uneven edge at bottom to make the bottom square.

f. Use the cut off pieces to fill in areas at the top to make the piece a rectangle.

h. If desired, use the cut off ends to add "fringe" to your tapestry.

g. When you have your final tapestry design, fuse it once more onto a clear background. Note: after this fusing, you can cut the piece into a circle and firepolish the edges if you choose.

h. If you added fringe to the piece, cut off the excess clear
   background with a wet ring saw to make the ends appear free.

3. Glass Tapestry Kiln Programs

Ramp 1: 300 degrees/hour up to 1000 degrees

Ramp 2: 1500 degrees/hour up to 1400 degrees

Ramp 3: 9999 degrees/hour down to 1000 degrees

Ramp 4: 150 degrees/hour down to 900 degrees

Hold: 1 hour.

Ramp 5: 150 degrees/hour down to 300 degrees

Program is complete.

Wait to open kiln until temperature is 150 degrees or lower.

4. Pitfalls

a. Strips break during cutting.
   With a sharp blade, make cuts with the tile saw slowly. Also, be sure glass is   well supported near the blade.

b. The stringers melt together and lose their thread-like quality.
   If the glass is placed close to the kiln coils, it may fuse more than just a tack at 1400 degrees. In this case, place it lower in the kiln, or lower your tack fuse temperature to 1380 degrees. Also, remember that transparent glass tends to melt at a lower temperature than opalescent.

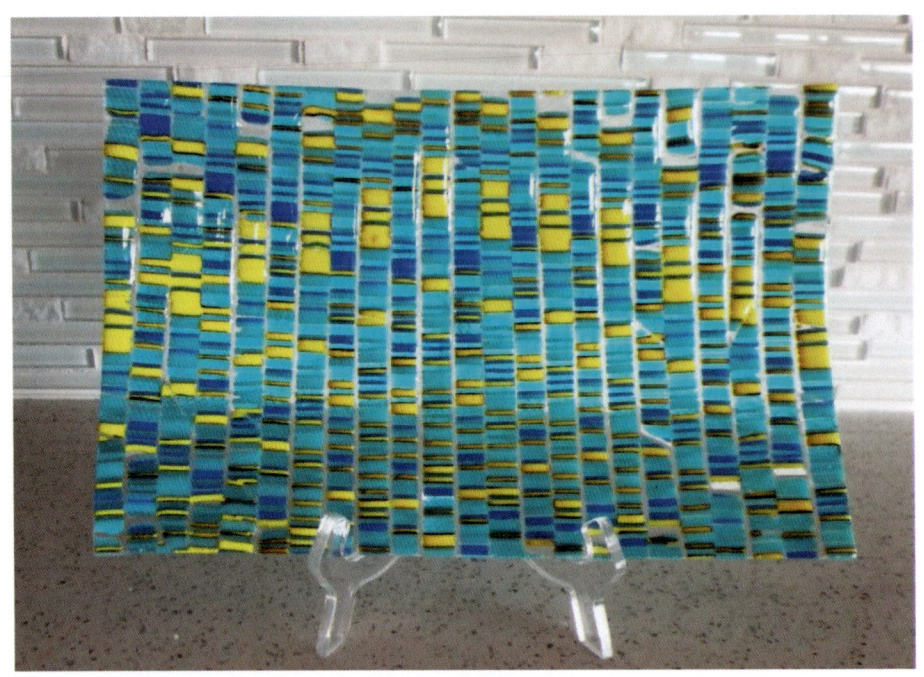

A dull saw blade and poor glass support caused the glass to break in several places as the strips were cut.

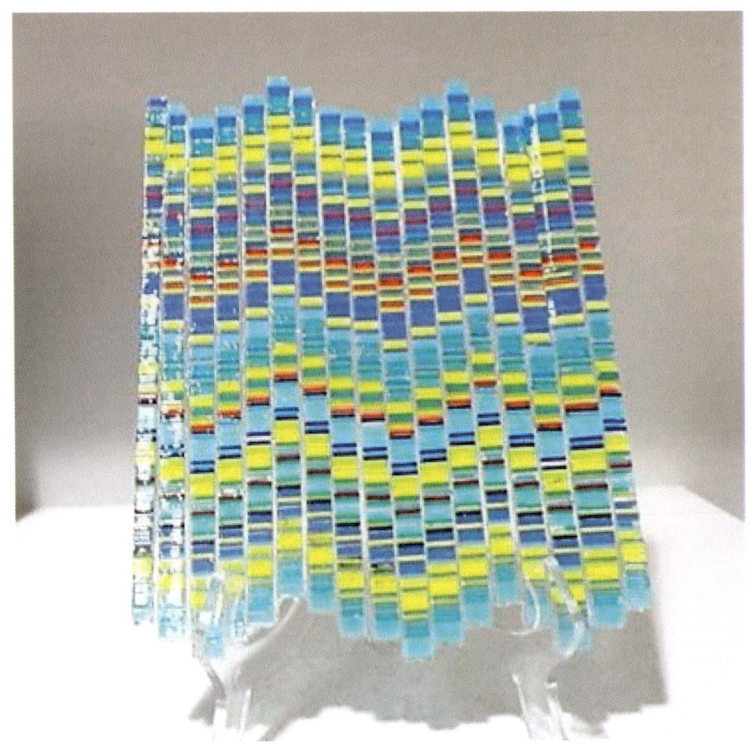

Stringers melted and lost some individuality

5. Results

****

Chapter 18: Dropout Vases and Cups

The drop-out vase is relatively easy to make. The idea is to place a disc or square of glass (previously fused if more than one layer of glass is used) on top of a donut shaped mold and heat it up. As the glass heats, the portion of glass over the hole sags through the hole and forms a vase or cup.

1. Equipment for Sagging Into a Drop-Out Mold
   a. Glass circle or square about ½"to 1" smaller in diameter than the diameter of the mold

b. Round or square mold with donut hole in the center

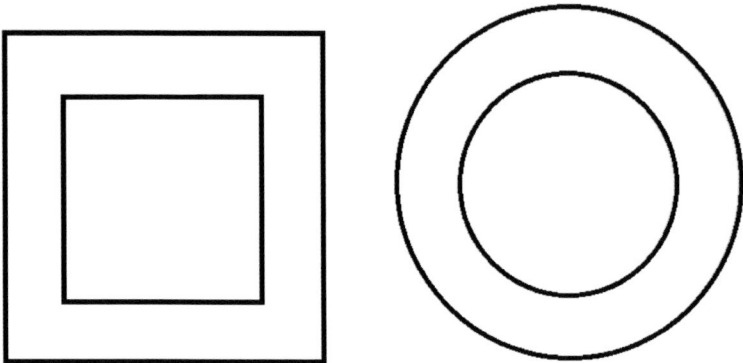

A square drop out mold   A round drop out mold.

   c. Kiln posts to elevate the donut mold off the shelf

   d. Prepared and programmed kiln

2. Process
   a. Prepare a donut mold with shelf primer to prevent the glass from sticking.
   b. Prepare a circle or square of glass slightly smaller than the outer diameter of the mold.

   Note: Keep in mind that in order to avoid the glass becoming too thin, plan for roughly 1 thickness of glass per 1-2" of drop through.

   c. Sag the glass through the hole using a kiln program which is slow and low temperature.

   Note: You will need to observe the glass as it changes around 1300 degrees. Be sure to wear didymium glasses and Kevlar gloves.
   d. When sagging is complete, advance the kiln to the next program

ramp.

3. Drop Out Vase Kiln Program

A typical sagging program for drop out vases is nearly the same as a draping program:

Ramp 1: 300°F/hour up to 1330°F

Ramp 2: 1000°F/hour down to 1000°

Ramp 3: 150°F/hour down to 900°F

Hold at 900°F for 1 ½ hours

Ramp 4: 300°F/hour down to 300°F

Program is complete.

Do not open the kiln until it reaches 150°F or below.

4. Pitfalls

a. Over sagging.
Oops! If it sags too far through the hole, you may end up with an interesting paperweight.

b. Under sagging.
The bottom doesn't reach the kiln shelf.

c. The vase is top heavy and falls over easily.

d. The glass is too thin where it has sagged.

 Here the glass is so thin that it separated along the line between glass colors.

e. The glass runs over the mold rim and gets stuck.
(See Chapter 8 for removing glass undercuts.)

5. Results

Results of sagging glass through a drop out mold can vary remarkably. Most results look something like the picture at the start of this chapter. A top heavy vase with a folded glass bottom and a long thin center stem usually result.

The vase looks somewhat better when it is not dropped from quite as high, but the rim remains heavily present.

Occasionally, dropping the glass from very high up has wonderful results. For this flower, I fused petals to a green disc and placed the flat flower on top of the donut mold. I placed tall posts on the kiln shelf under the donut and let the flower drop through the hole until it began to tip up ready to fall through completely. A large green blob of folded glass sat on the shelf under the mold when it was done. When I lifted up the flower, the folded glass at the bottom broke off and I was left with just the stem of the flower. Serendipity!

****

"Whether you take the doughnut hole as a blank space or as an entity unto itself is a purely metaphysical question and does not affect the taste of the doughnut one bit."

Haruki Murakami, <u>A Wild Sheep Chase</u>

Chapter 19: Removing Rims on Tall Vessels

For years I wanted to be able to remove the rims from drop-out vessels, but I couldn't figure out how to do it. Finally, I saw some vases on Instagram in 2017 which had the rims removed, so I knew it was hypothetically possible. When I inquired of the artist how she did it, she said after the drop fusing, she scored the vase and broke off the thick rim with a hammer! I was **very** impressed, but extremely fearful that my vases would end up in shards on my workbench.

Not long ago I saw something on Youtube which was a revelation. A woman removed the rim from a drop out vase with a Dremel while the vase was turned on a lazysusan! Brilliant! Now, here was a technique I might be able to master.

1. Equipment to Remove Rims

    a. Previously dropped-though vase with rim still attached

    b.Turntable of some kind.

        1) Lapidary tables are the most preferred but also the most expensive turntables I have seen. ($1100 or more)

        2) A plastic lazysusan from the housewares department at the grocery store is the least expensive, but you must have a water source and be able to turn it with your third hand.

        3) Because I mostly work alone and only have two hands, I compromised by getting a small potter's wheel for about $350. I placed an aquarium-type sump pump from the hardware store in the basin. Finally, I added a beaded water distribution tube I got

online to the pump and voila! I had a self-turning, self-wetting table for my vase.

c. A Dremel or similar rotary tool with a wide diamond blade on a long flexible shaft

d. Also helpful: a lapidary disc.

Note: I glued my lapidary disc to a magnetic backing and placed it on my potter's wheel. This makes a much less expensive lapidary machine which also has a water distribution system. Imperfections with the top edge of the vase can be ground off easily.

2. Process to Remove Rims
      a. Invert your big-rimmed vase so it sits upside down on top of your lazysusan.
      b. Turn on the water flow so that the region of the vase where you want your cut to be is constantly getting wet.
      c. Slowly spin the lazysusan while holding gently onto the vase.
      d. In your free hand, hold the Dremel vertically and softly touch it to the spinning vase. A score line will form.
      e. Continue scoring along the same line until the vase separates from the rim. This will take several minutes.
      f. Finish any rough spots where the Dremel hopped by using your glass grinder followed by the lapidary disc.

g. Polish the top edge with lapping compound on the lapidary disc or with a polisher drill bit if desired.

3. Kiln Program (See previous chapter to fuse the drop-out vase.)

4. Pitfalls

   a. Same as those of drop-outs.

   b. Glass breaks when cut on thin area just below rim. When this happens, use your grinder to create a beveled lip for the top of the vase. Finish it off with the lapidary disc to make it smooth.

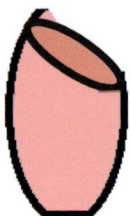

5. Results

   The results speak for themselves.

****

"Your positive action combined with positive thinking results in success."

Shiv Khera

Chapter 20: Combing Glass

Combing or raking, as it is sometimes called, creates a thrilling new way to manipulate hot glass. The results are sometimes spectacular, and the process always is! The artist is quite literally manipulating the glass at a temperature of about 1700 degrees Fahrenheit! Unlike glass blowing where the blowing is done on a pipe outside the kiln, with combing, the hot glass stays inside the kiln. It is so much fun to push and pull the thick, syrupy glass to generate curves and swirls. The danger of the process creates its own appeal too!

1. Equipment for Combing Glass

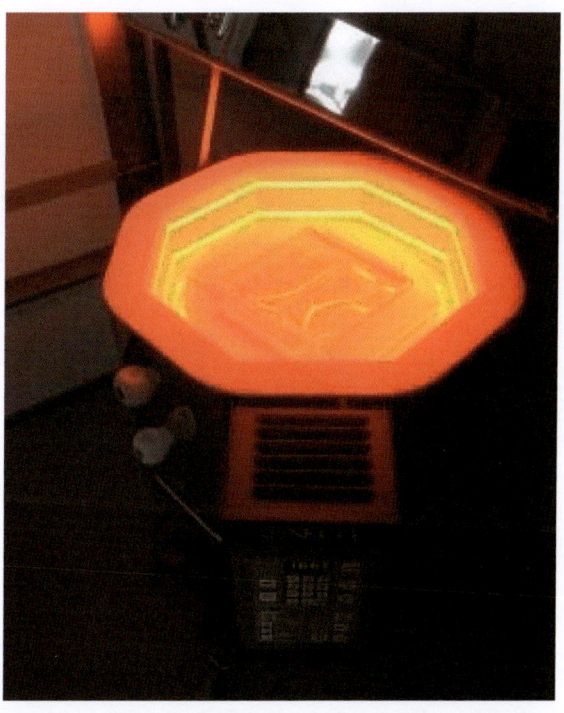

Kiln opened at 1700 degrees Fahrenheit for combing.

Combing glass creates a great potential for accidental burns. Seventeen hundred degrees Fahrenheit is incredibly hot. Paper burns at about 450 degrees. (Remember the old sci-fi book by Ray Bradbury called <u>Fahrenheit 451</u> wherein all books were burned?) We have all been singed once or twice by a hot match or a lighter.

The kiln at combing temperature is far, far hotter and as such, deserves much respect and caution. Therefore, most of the equipment needed for combing revolves around this need for safety. The kiln lid will be opened to work the glass when its temperature is at its peak, but the handle is much too hot to hold without heavy duty Kevlar gloves or better, a hands-free lifting system.

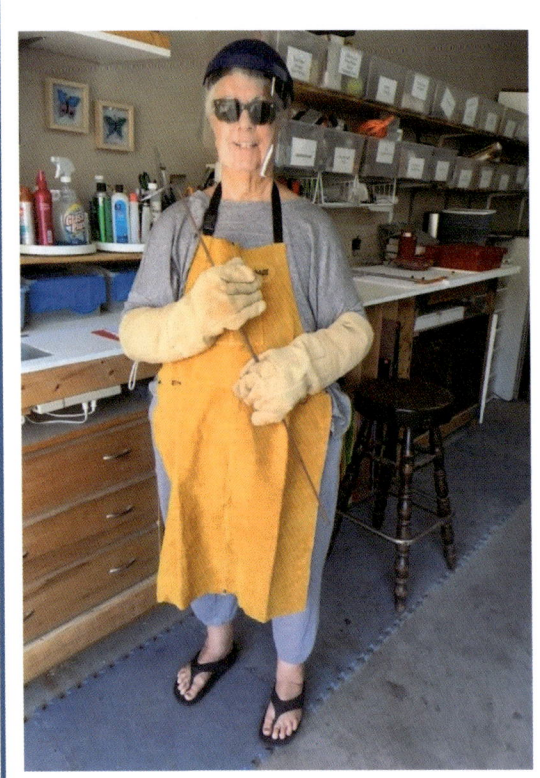

From: "Grandma's Glass Fusing Fashions:

The Combing Collection."

a. Clear face protector

b. Didymium eye glasses

c.   Leather welder's apron

d. Long Kevlar gloves

e. Long sleeved all-cotton shirt and pants

f. Stainless steel bent and pointed rod

If you don't want singed eyebrows or burned forearms, please protect yourself when raking glass! Wear all cotton clothing as it won't stick to the skin the way plastic fabrics like polyester will if they get hot. And be careful!

It is difficult to open the hot kiln lid with Kevlar gloves on, so my husband, the ever helpful engineer, rigged up a hoist system to lift the kiln lid when combing glass. It works like a dream and, "Look Ma, no hands!" I highly recommend such a system (and such a husband) if you can arrange it.

Hoist on the ceiling

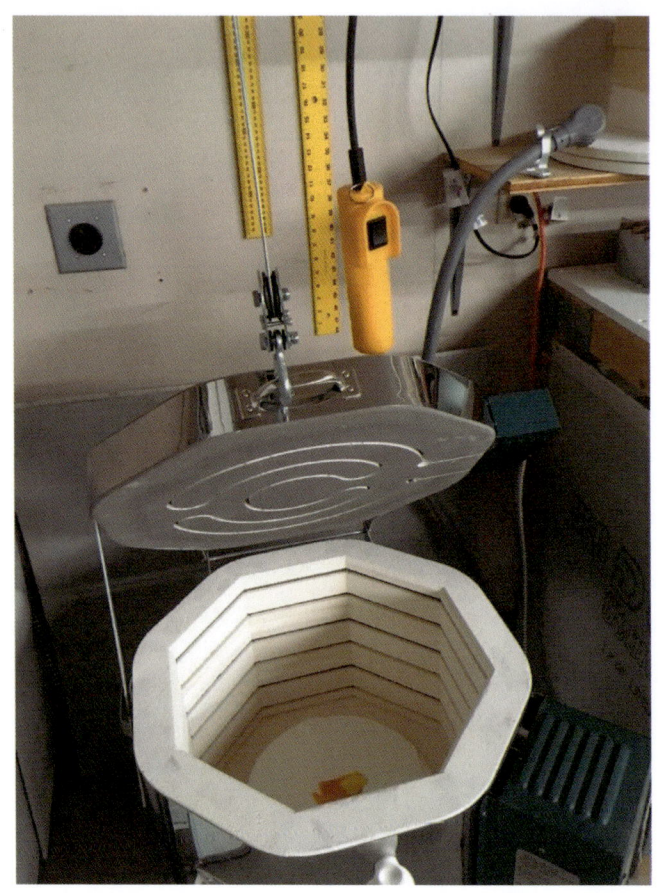

An electric lid hoist is mounted on the garage ceiling.

The yellow control box is suspended above the lid. The control box was getting too warm above the kiln, so after this picture was taken, I hooked a bungee cord to it and moved it to the side where it works fine.

2. Process of Combing Glass

The process of combing glass is conceptually quite simple. Heat up the glass, comb it, and then cool it down. Heating the glass without burning yourself and planning a nice design are the real challenges here. So how do you design it?

a. The most common design technique is a series of strips in varying colors placed on edge tightly together. Hint: Using several strips of clear glass between colors makes the individual colors stand out and look vibrant. It also shows a nice 3-dimensional effect. Pick your colors to produce the effect you want. Colored strips do not need to extend the entire width across the piece, but you will need to fill in empty areas with clear or another color. Plan now just how many times and where you will push or pull the glass.

b. Cut enough 9 inch long strips about 3/8 inch or 1/2 inch wide to make a 9 inch square. Using tack glue or hairspray to stick them together into a big stack makes them easier to move around onto the fiber blanketed shelf.

Strips cut and glued before for heating.

c. Place fiber blanketed kiln bricks on each side of the square on the shelf to keep the glass from expanding when heated. Note: In the picture, I arranged them first as a square in an old cake pan with the bottom cut off. Before I fused the strips, however, I removed the pan and replaced it with firebricks on each side to make removal easier after combing. Bottomless molds may also be purchased.

d. Heat up the kiln. When the temperature reaches 1700-1750 degrees and begins its Hold cycle, wait a few minutes to be sure the glass is as hot as the kiln. Then open up the lid *CAREFULLY*. Only open the lid as far as needed to comb your piece, but take care not to touch the combing rod to the kiln coils. This may cause you a shock or may cause the coils to short out. The heat will be intense, so be sure you are wearing an outfit from 'Grandma's Combing Collection' and use a lift of some kind to open the lid.

e. Work quickly to push and pull the glass into your design. The glass will feel like you are combing through very thick syrup or taffy. You only have a minute or less before the glass will become hard on the surface and too cool to comb. If this happens before your design is finished, close the lid and wait for the temperature to rise again to 1700 degrees before reopening it and continuing to comb. Repeat this step as often as needed.

f. As soon as you are finished combing the glass, close the lid and advance your kiln to the next Ramp.

g. Cool the glass completely. If desired, you can cold work and slump your piece after the cool down period.

h. The chances are good that you will not be completely satisfied with the appearance of the edges of your piece. It will have fiber blanket marks and need some finishing work.

3. Kiln Program for Combing Glass

Ramp 1: 500 degrees/hour up to 1000 degrees

Ramp 2: 1500 degrees/hour up to 1700-1750 degrees
If you have a clam shell kiln, 1700 degrees will be enough, but you may need to raise the temp a bit if you have a regular studio glass kiln.

Note: You need a kiln which uses 240 volts to be able to comb glass. A 120 volt kiln will be unable to generate enough heat for this process.

Hold for 1-2 hours. Advance to Ramp 3 when combing is finished.

Ramp 3: 9999 degrees/hour down to 1000 degrees

Ramp 4: 150 degrees/hour down to 900 degrees

Hold 1 ½ -2 hours.

Ramp 5: 300 degrees/hour down to 400 degrees

The program is complete, but wait to open the kiln until temperature reads 150 degrees or below.

4. Pitfalls of Glass Combing

    a. Difficulty making curves.

Straight lines forward and back are usually easy, but side to side and curves are difficult unless you are a body builder or unless the glass is 1700 degrees or more. *Keep the glass hot to make curves easier.* You may need to raise the temperature to 1750 degrees for CoE90 glass. Be sure to hold the glass at peak temperature for a few minutes before you begin to comb it to be sure it is as hot as the kiln. For CoE96 glass, a somewhat lower temperature around 1680-1700 may be enough to make those lovely sweeps in the glass.

    b. Fiber blanket stuck in the glass.

When the glass is very hot, the steel combing rod has a tendency to dig deeply into the glass. While this is not necessarily a bad thing in terms of design, it is possible to pick up some of the fiber blanket into the glass. This is not a good thing. This happens especially if the glass is getting cooler and you find yourself pushing or pulling harder to make your design. Avoid this by stopping, closing the kiln, letting it reheat, and trying again. It can also happen if you are too aggressive when the glass is at its peak temperature. In this case, lighten up your pressure of the combing rod.

Oops! You can also get fiber blanket stuck by beginning your combing beyond the edge of the glass! (In my defense, it's hard to see well in a very hot kiln.)

c. Glass sticks to the rod.

When the rod gets too hot while combing, the molten glass may stick to it. If this happens, lift the rod off the glass, and carefully immerse it in a bucket of water before resuming combing. The cold water will cause the glass to break off the rod.

d. Not digging deeply enough with the comb.

If the glass is not hot enough, the combing rod will tend to skim the glass surface only. It may skip across the surface leaving only minor marks where a deeper impact was desired. In this case, stop, close the kiln lid, wait until the kiln heats up, and retry combing.

My first try

The raking here was done on glass that wasn't quite hot enough to get good penetration with the rake. You can see where the first strokes at the top were reasonably good draws, but in the final stroke at the bottom the rod barely skimmed the surface.

e. The molten glass flows to one side of the shelf.

This happens when the shelf is not level. Use a small bubble level to determine if the shelf is level prior to turning on the kiln. Note the position of the bubble in the center of the level in at least four places on the shelf.

I had a sliding problem here because the kiln shelf wasn't level. I cut off the edge of glass where thinning occurred. The colors compressed so much that you would never believe that I had two thicknesses of clear between each of the color strips in this one!

    f. Burns.

        As mentioned earlier, burns and fire are real concerns when dealing with the high temperatures of combing glass. It is imperative that the artist protect him/herself as well as the studio area. Protective clothing and a bucket of water at the ready are essential parts of the combing experience.

    g. Eye damage.

        Anytime a hot kiln is opened, eye protection is a must. Didymium glasses or a welder's mask do a good job of preventing permanent retinal damage and vision loss. Always wear them if you plan to open the hot kiln.

5. Results

A nice 3-D effect in this one was achieved by placing 3 clear strips beside each colored strip.

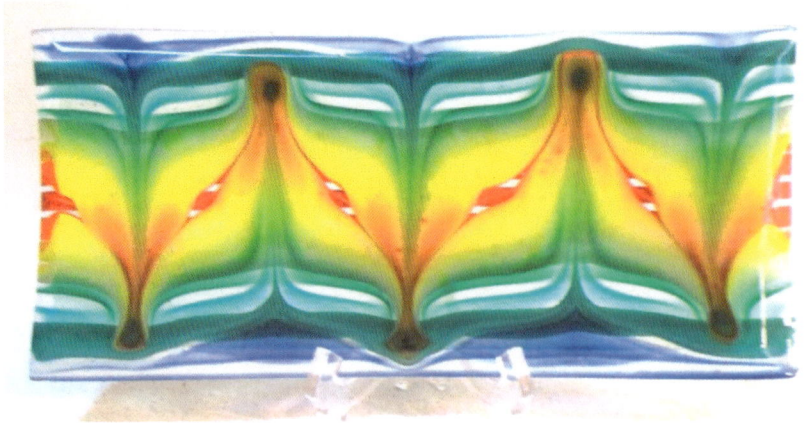

The yellow went wild in this one. Not sure why, but it kind of looks like wolf faces or whale's tales, doesn't it?

Combed, sliced and put back together just for a fun effect

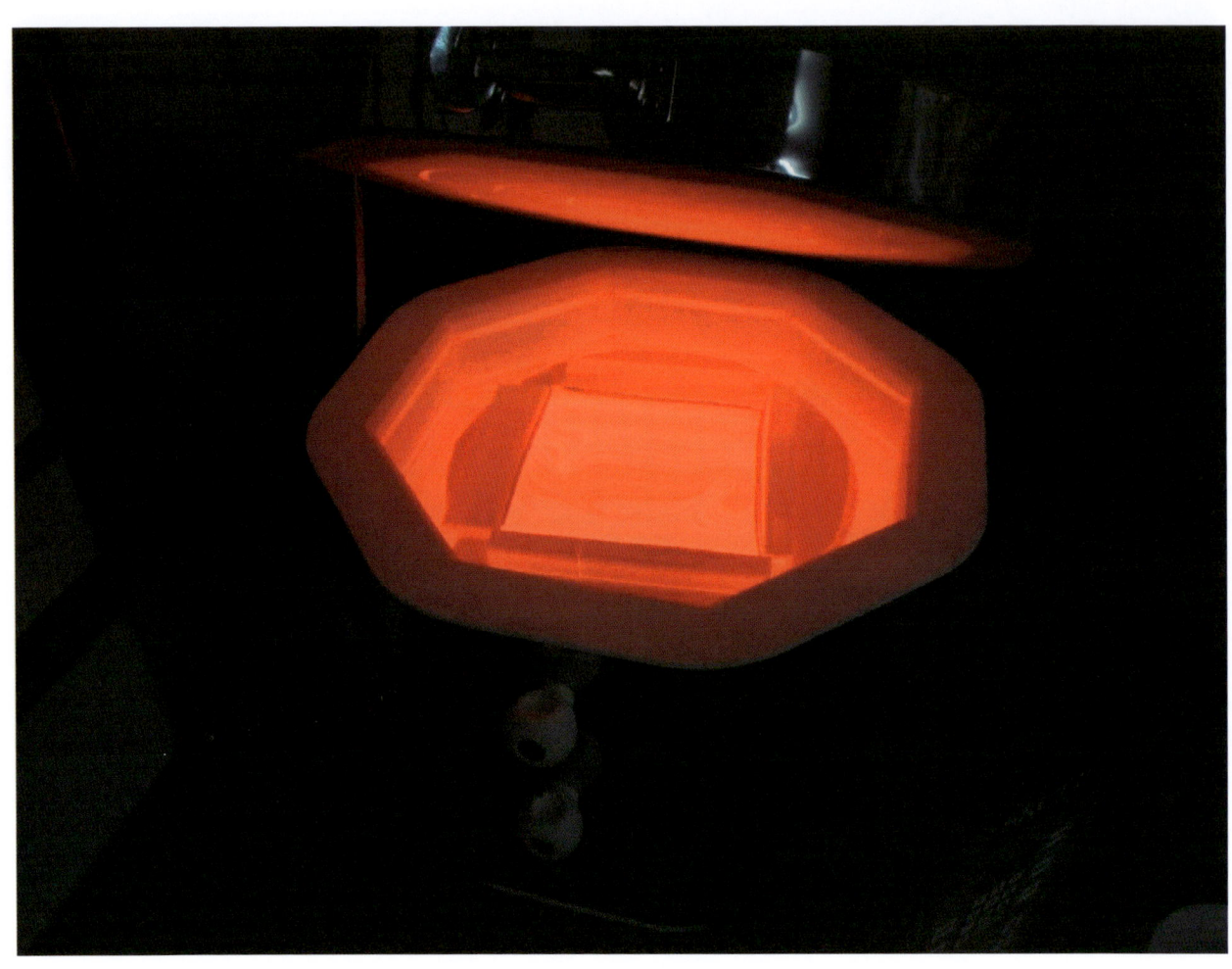

And please remember, the open kiln is *HOT!*

****

Chapter 21: Finishing Touches

The devil is in the details, it is said. So too, it is with glass work. Very often a piece is a bit rough looking when the fusing is done. A bit of spit and polish is needed to make your objet d'art perfect and ready for display, sale, or gifting.

1. Smooth Grinding

When grinding glass to a smooth edge, or surface, always start with a coarse grit diamond pad and work progressively to finer and finer ones.

A precautionary note: Remove any diamond rings you might normally wear before grinding anything with a diamond pad. This prevents scratching your jewelry!

A few turns of the grinder on a lapidary wheel can work wonders to smooth out rough edges, but sometimes, the edge is too rough or time is too short to wait for the wheel to work its magic. In these cases the answer may be using the wet saw or glass grinder to smooth out the edges followed by fire polishing.

2. Beveling.

If your glass piece is very thick, as happens with multiple layers, you may want to bevel the edges and make it appear thinner. This is easily accomplished using a beveling jig for the wet saw followed by fire polishing. Take care to bevel each side the same for best results.

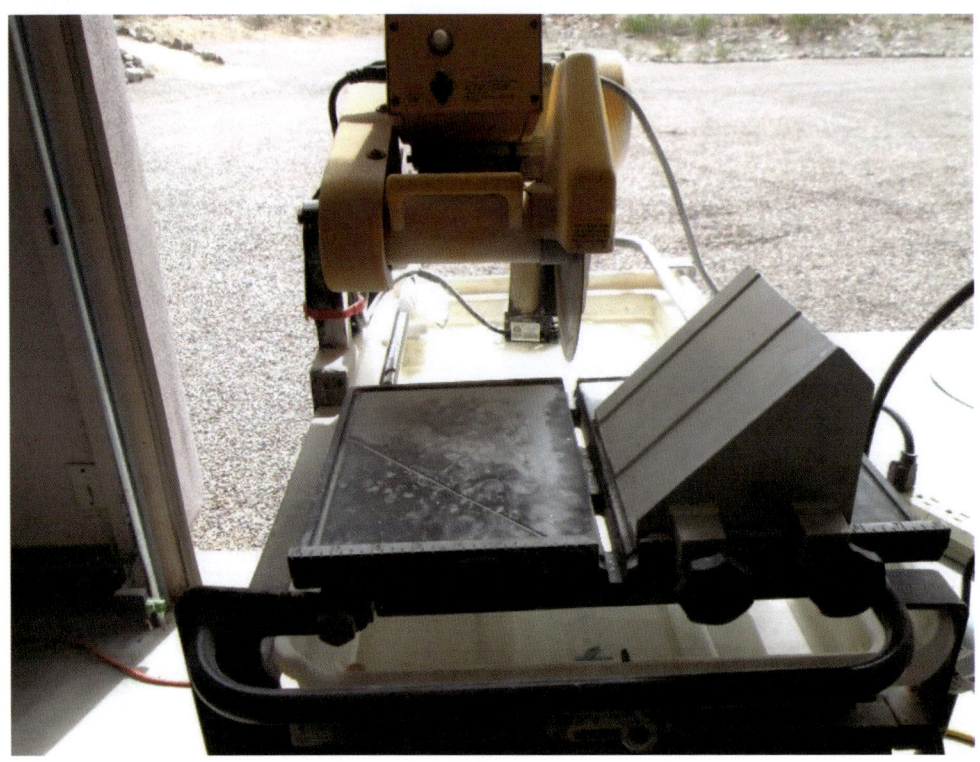

Wet saw with bevel jig. (Made for ceramic tiles, the saw works perfectly well for glass if a diamond-edged blade is used.)

3. Fire Polishing

If white or sharp edges remain on your piece when you are finished cold working it, it may need to be fire polished. To remove the white only, heat it up in the kiln to about 1300 degrees Fahrenheit. This is hotter than the temperatures needed for slumping, draping, or sagging. These processes should be done *after* fire polishing to avoid distorting your piece.

To round off the sharp corners, glass needs to be heated a bit hotter, to about 1375-1400 degrees. Each time you heat up the glass, even for fire polishing, remember to follow a normal kiln program of heating and cooling including annealing. Just how long the fire polishing program will take depends, of course, on how big and how thick your glass is.

****

"Whatever it takes to finish things, finish. You will learn more from a glorious failure than you ever will from something you never finished."
Neil Gaiman

Part III: Making It Real

Chapter 22: Managing Expenses

1. Ways to save money

   a. Kiln

   The kiln is the most expensive piece of equipment needed to fuse glass. Costs   can range from hundreds to thousands of dollars. Sometimes a person can find a used one online. The fuser might also be able to rent time on a kiln from another fuser or at a "paint your own ceramics" store. Art schools also offer possibilities for use of a kiln. By taking courses in fusing, a person may be able to connect with others and find kiln time this way. Creative thinking can solve this problem, often without the big expenditure of a kiln.

   b. Tools

   Start your fusing career with only the minimum tools needed and gradually add to your collection as you need more tools.

   c. Power

   Many power companies offer time of use plans wherein power costs more or less depending upon the time of day. Switching to this type of plan with your power company will benefit your pocketbook. Most kilns are well insulated and will not lose much heat into your home. Planning your program so as to raise the temperature in your kiln during the cheapest time of day will save you considerable cash.

   d. Use Your Expensive Leftover Scraps.

Glass fusing creates scraps, some large enough to cut again and some very small. Glass is expensive. It is important to make use of as much of it as possible, leaving little as waste. Here are some ideas of how to use those small glass tidbits to make beautiful artsy things.

It is easy to scatter glass scraps onto a base layer of glass and make something lovely.

It is also easy to cut small leftover pieces into strips and make a rainbow.

Or an Easter basket can be made by casually arranging the leftover strips on a square of glass and draping it over an inverted cup mold (or cocktail shaker).

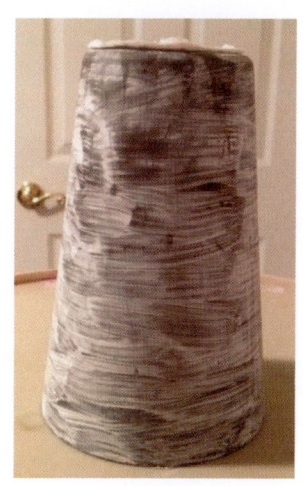

e. Dots

Small dots are easy to make. They can be used to apply points to designs or used in jewelry as shown below. Make dots by layering two small roughly ¼ - ½ inch squares of glass. Fuse to 1550°F. Small domes will result.

i. Melting Scraps

If you have a lot of leftover pieces, making a new piece of glass is a possibility. There are two easy ways to do this: screen melting and pot melting. Screen melting produces a bit more marbled appearance in the glass while pot melting produces a more homogeneous color on the glass surface.

Screen melted

With kiln posts.

Without kiln posts.

In addition to putting fiber paper on the shelf surface, it is important to put fiber paper around the inside of the ring to prevent the glass sticking. The screen should not be coated with kiln release.

The steel screen and the steel ring may both chip during cooling. This chipping is called spalling. The chips may cover the surface of the newly fused glass, but as soon as the glass is lifted from the kin, the spall falls off leaving only the layer of glass.

When screen melting or pot melting, the black in dark colors becomes very pronounced. Even light glass colors become much darker in these processes. The glass used should be of mostly light colors and mixed with large amounts of clear or white scraps for the best results.

j. Pot melting.

Pot melting is another way to melt down little glass scraps. In this case, a ceramic pot is lifted above the ring. About 3 pounds of glass pieces are placed in the pot such that they will not spill over the pot sides when melted. The temperature is raised with two soaks as it rises. A soak at about 1000°F for an hour will assure that all the glass is 1000°F and not just the outer glass. Then another hold at 1650°F for about an hour will allow enough time for nearly all the glass to flow through the hole(s) at the bottom of the pot. An inexpensive, unglazed garden pot with its single hole can easily be used for pot melting.

Other pots which have multiple holes of various shapes are available for pot melting from glass stores.

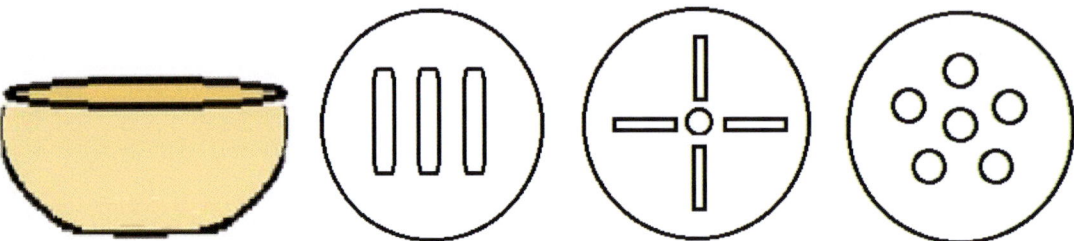

Some hole designs.

The pot is elevated over the ring in a similar fashion to the screen in screen melting.

The same cautions must be used when pot melting as with screen melting. Fiber paper or fiber blanket must be used around the inside of the ring and on the kiln shelf. Also, use of dark glass should be minimized. An abundance of clear or white will produce the best results.

2. Ways to Make Money

a. Online.

You don't need your own website to market your glass for sale. Social websites such as Facebook, Instagram and others make it easy to put a picture of your glass art up for anyone to see. You can include a description as well as a price and contact information. Try starting a blog about your art and see if it catches on. Include lots of pictures.

Ebay, Amazon, Craigslist and similar sites are also places where you can market your pieces. These websites may charge a small fee for use, but selling on these sites will reach many, many people and help your sales, thus making the cost bearable.

Getting a domain name and setting up your own web page is another option chosen by many. Multiple sites offer expertise in development of your own website. It is imperative that you become listed with Google, Yahoo, or some similar service such that when a potential buyer of your art wants to search for you, he will be able to find you.

b. Tent Shows.

Art festivals are a good way to get the local community aware and interested in your art. Be sure to have business cards available at check out so that people can pass them along to friends. Be aware that tent shows generally are not without cost.

c. Consignment.

Often it is possible to market your art in glass stores. The store may take a percentage of your sales price, but will display it nicely. Art galleries and jewelry stores are other sites you will want to investigate. Any store which displays and sells art is a possibility. Do the legwork and it may pay off in unexpected ways. Five no's today doesn't mean you won't have a yes tomorrow.

d. Marketing.

Reading a marketing book or taking a marketing course will help you find other ways to improve sales of your lovely art. Believe in yourself. If you think it's beautiful, it is. If someone wants to buy it, it's sublime!

****

Waste not; want not.

Ben Franklin

Chapter 23: The Philosophical Perspective

Fusing glass is both an art form and a science. In my experience, many great scientists are also great artists. The benefits to humanity are incalculable from both areas of study. To fully utilize both the left and right brains to their maximum ability is a marvelous thing which results in great advancement of the human condition.

Unfortunately, I am neither a great artist nor a great scientist. I have degrees in science but am by no means a particular talent there. I wanted a degree in art, but I soon discovered I had no particular genius in that arena either. What I do have is a desire to organize and share the concepts and skills I have learned.

They say those who can't do, teach. For 25 years, I taught what little I knew about science in universities. All the while, I knew that the facts I was teaching were probably obsolete soon after I taught them. What I hoped was that the concepts and ways of approaching the subjects were perpetual.

The same is true for art. I have written these books in an effort to share what I have learned about fusing glass in the hope that basic concepts and ways of thinking about fusing glass will be eternal. I hope that those people who have true artistic genius will be able to use what my books teach to create new and evocative glass pieces to thrill the world. Thank you all for giving us your wondrous art!

****

Appendices

Appendix A: Melting Points of Metals

Adding metal to a piece you are fusing can add that element of surprise which transforms a piece from ordinary to spectacular. It is important to know which metals will work, however, and for this you need to know their melting points. If the melting point is too low, the metal will liquefy and evaporate during fusing. It may also give off toxic fumes. Some melting points of metals are:

Aluminum: 1221°F

Copper: 1984°F

Steel: 2500°F

Iron: 2750 °F

Silver: 176°F

Gold: 1948°F

Platinum: 3224°F

Metals are used in the making of colored glass. If you have ever watched a glassblower, you may have seen him dip the molten glass into some powdered metal to give it a color. If you are using them in fused glass, however, the best way to add most metals is to fuse them between glass layers as "inclusions." Be sure to clean the metal very thoroughly to eliminate any oils before fusing.

Appendix B: Temperature Conversion Chart

° Fahrenheit	°Celsius
150	65.56
200	93.33
300	14.89
930	498.89
1000	537.78
1100	593.33
1200	648.89
1221	660.56
1225	662.78
1300	704.44
1350	732.22
1400	760
1405	762
1420	771
1500	815.56
1600	871.1
1625	885
1700	926.67
1763	961.67
1800	982.2
1948	1084.44
1984	1084.44
2000	1093.3
2300	1260
2500	1371.11
2750	1510
3224	1773.33

About the Author

April Calmelat began working with stained glass windows in the 1990s after being inspired by the lovely cathedral windows of Europe. In 1996, she bought her first kiln and began to explore the warm glass medium. Captivated, she has been exploring different fusing techniques ever since. She considers herself a serious hobbyist rather than a specialist in the medium, as she loves to try new things. She works in her garage in Phoenix, Arizona.

Printed in Great Britain
by Amazon

13633483R00107